AT THE ORIGINS OF CHRISTIAN WORSHIP

At the Origins of Christian Worship

The Context and Character of Earliest Christian Devotion

Larry W. Hurtado

WILLIAM B. EERDMANS PUBLISHING COMPANY
GRAND RAPIDS, MICHIGAN / CAMBRIDGE, U.K.

First published 1999 in the U.K. by Paternoster Press
Paternoster Press is an imprint of Paternoster Publishing
P.O. Box 300, Carlisle, Cumbria, CA3 0QS, UK

This edition published 2000 in the United States of America by
Wm. B. Eerdmans Publishing Company
255 Jefferson Ave. S.E., Grand Rapids, Michigan 49503 /
P.O. Box 163, Cambridge CB3 9PU U.K.
www.eerdmans.com

Printed in the United States of America

05 04 03 02 01   7 6 5 4 3 2

Library of Congress Cataloging-in-Publication Data

Hurtado, Larry W., 1943-
At the origins of Christian worship : the context and character
of earliest Christian devotion / Larry Hurtado.
p.   cm.
Originally published: Carlisle, Cumbria, UK :
Paternoster Press, 1999.
Includes bibliographical references.
ISBN 0-8028-4749-8 (pbk. : alk. paper)
1. Worship — History — Early church, ca. 30-600.   I. Title.
BV6.H87   2000
264'.011 — dc21

00-041735

to

Shannon

Contents

Preface

It is an honour to have been invited to deliver the 1999 Didsbury Lectures at the British Isles Nazarene College, Manchester. This book incorporates my four lectures, here lightly edited for publication, as well as an introduction, notes and a list of works cited. The first three chapters explore historical questions about the earliest Christian worship and focus on the Roman setting of earliest Christianity and the character of its worship in this religious environment. These chapters reflect lines of investigation that I have been following for a number of years. I have attempted to make this discussion accessible to any interested reader, but I also hope that it makes some contribution to our historical grasp of early Christian devotion.

In the final chapter I offer some reflections on Christian worship today. Candid self-disclosure by scholars is now perhaps more acceptable than in some previous times, but may still be uncomfortable to some. In a subject such as early Christianity, it stretches credibility for scholars to claim to have no personal stake. We can, however, aim for accuracy in presenting the data and even more so in referring to the views of those with whom we disagree. Moreover, we can always seek simply to understand patiently and sympathetically. Perhaps some readers who regard any religious faith as incompatible with critical scholarship may regard me as perverse in admitting to the hope that a jury of fair-minded citizens would be able to convict me on the charge of being a Christian. (I also admit, however, that there are days when my behaviour might very well enable a good defence counsel to get me off the charge!)

But, whatever the personal stance of my readers, I hope that the treatment of historical questions in chapters 1–3 will be of some value for anyone interested in the origins of Christianity. Chapter 4, though concerned with the contemporary practice of Christian worship, may be of some interest to non-participant observers of Christianity as well as to adherents.

I take sole responsibility for the following pages, but I also wish to acknowledge Troy Miller, one of my Ph.D. students, who read chapter one and offered helpful comments. Some of the ideas presented in these lectures have also been discussed with colleagues in the Faculty of Divinity here, particularly Nick Wyatt (the Graeco-Roman 'pagan' background) and Peter Hayman (the Jewish background). Since my move to Edinburgh in 1996, I have been privileged to be a part of the vigorous group of scholars that make up the Faculty of Divinity/New College team, and I am most grateful for their welcome and comradeship. These are especially meaningful coming from a collection of colleagues who hold vigorously a variety of scholarly views and who represent a diversity of personal stances on questions of religious faith.

Chapter three is an adapted version of an invited paper presented to the International Conference on the Historical Origins of the Worship of Jesus held at St. Andrews University, 13–17 June 1998. The paper will also appear in the edited volume of essays from that conference. I thank the editors of that volume, Dr. James Davila and Dr. Carey Newman, as well as the publishers, E. J. Brill, for permission to use the paper here also.

In December 1998 my wife, Shannon, and I celebrated our twentieth wedding anniversary. These have been twenty years of warm and loving companionship, all the more comforting because these years have not been without their demands and difficulties. Though she is heavily involved in her own research into nineteenth-century British cultural and art history, she has always shown patient and helpful interest in the topics of my studies as well. To her I dedicate this book, with gratitude and love.

New College, Edinburgh

Abbreviations

Abbreviations of books of the Bible, Apocrypha, Philo, Josephus and extra-canonical early Christian writings are those of the *Journal of Biblical Literature*.

ANF *The Ante-Nicene Fathers*, eds. Roberts and Donaldson

BCE Before the Common Era

CE Common Era

CEV Contemporary English Version

HE *The Ecclesiastical History*, Eusebius.

JB Jerusalem Bible

JTS *Journal of Theological Studies*

LXX Septuagint

MM *The Vocabulary of the Greek Testament Illustrated from the Papyri and other Non-Literary Sources*, by Moulton and Milligan.

NAB New American Bible

NEB New English Bible

NIV New International Version

NRSV New Revised Standard Version

NT New Testament

NTS *New Testament Studies*

OT Old Testament

RGG *Die Religion in Geschichte und Gegenwart*, ed. K. Galling

Introduction

Christian worship has a long and complex history, and this little volume is about its earliest observable stages. Over the last two decades my own research has focused on the first two centuries of the Christian movement, with special attention to the origins and early development of devotion to Christ. I have been particularly interested in the expression of this devotion in the worship setting. I am, however, a specialist in the New Testament and Christian origins, not a historian of liturgy; but I have given considerable attention to ancient Christian worship because of its significance for understanding early Christianity. At the risk of severe understatement, one of the characteristic things early Christians did was to worship. Early Christianity was, after all, a religious movement, striving to orient adherents to the divine purposes proclaimed in its gospel message. If, therefore, we want to analyse major phenomena of early Christianity, Christians' devotional practices are clearly key matters for attention. But the worship of the earliest Christians casts light on other features of the Christian movement as well. In the following chapters I approach early Christian worship by setting it within the context of the Roman world (including particularly the Jewish tradition) in which it emerged.

Scholars of the New Testament and Christian origins have tended to focus on the religious beliefs of early Christians, and the data for their studies have tended to be the verbal expressions of beliefs in early Christian texts and the vocabulary of these expressions. The verbal expressions of early Christian beliefs, for example, their 'christology', are of course important. But in the intense scholarly investigation and debate, the big questions have been what these faith expressions *mean*. What, for example, did early Christians mean when they called Christ their 'lord'? The Greek and Aramaic terms translated by 'lord' can carry various meanings ranging from a polite address to a social superior (e.g., 'Sir', 'master') to designating a deity. I have argued that the devotional practice of early Christians is the crucial context for assessing the meaning of their verbal expressions of beliefs about Christ. Modern linguistics has helped us to see that words, which often have a complex and diverse range of meanings, acquire their specific meaning in the context in which they are used. I contend that the specific connotation of early Christian christological titles and devotional gestures is most clearly assessed by taking full account of the worship context in which they were used. For example, addressing Jesus as 'lord' in the worship setting, using the term to invoke and appeal to Jesus, connoted something far more precise and striking than the other more general semantic possibilities of the term 'lord'. It represented addressing him in the context and way that ancients addressed the deities that they gathered to worship. To refer to Jesus as 'lord' in other settings could connote something different, such as a recognition of him as master or as leader of his devotees. But to address him as 'lord' as a feature of the collective worship of early Christian groups indicates a much more precise and exalted meaning for the term.[1]

It also makes sense to take due account of the worship of early Christians because of the importance of worship in the Roman period as constituting and manifesting religion. In the ancient world especially, one's religion was understood and assessed in terms of how, when, and what one worshipped. Worship was seen as the characteristic and crucial expression of one's religious orientations and commitments. It

---

[1] I have offered an analysis of Paul's use of the *Kyrios* title, showing its varying contextual connotations, in Hurtado, 'Lord', in Hawthorne and Martin (eds.) *Dictionary of Paul and His Letters*, 560–69.

is a bit puzzling to me, therefore, that a good many scholars who profess a commitment to a historical understanding of early Christianity in its original setting have not always seen how important early Christian devotional practices and patterns are. To cite one illustration of this, among the complaints made about and against Christians in the first three centuries there is the recurrent charge that they disdain the worship of the traditional gods. Clearly, the ancient critics of Christians saw their cultic behaviour as a major and defining feature. When Christians were put on trial (as reflected, for example, in the famous letter of Pliny to Trajan, and in the *Martyrdom of Polycarp*), it was demanded that they perform certain *cultic* gestures, such as calling upon the gods, offering incense to the image of the Emperor and ritually cursing Jesus.[2] In any account of early Christianity that seeks to take account of the historical context, therefore, the devotional practices and scruples of Christians should be central.

In its ancient Roman context, two features in particular characterised and distinguished early Christian worship. First, it was exclusivist, with disdain for the worship of the many deities of the Roman environment, and, secondly, it involved devotion offered exclusively to the God of the Bible and to Christ. These two features are in fact eloquent indicators of the importance of the topic of this book and provide the logic for its content and for the lectures from which it arose. Thus the first two chapters take as their premise the exclusivity of early Christian worship in the context of the Roman world, while the third chapter focuses on what I term the 'binitarian shape' of earliest Christian worship, with God and Christ as the two exclusive recipients of the worship of believers who considered themselves to be true and devout monotheists.

In chapter 1 I sketch the Roman religious environment of Christians, especially those first-century Gentile Christians

---

[2] Pliny, *Epistles* 10.96 (text and commentary in Sherwin-White, *The Letters of Pliny*, 691–710); *Martyrdom of Polycarp* 8–9 (text and translation in Lightfoot, Harmer, and Holmes, *The Apostolic Fathers: Greek Texts and English Translations of their Writings*), 232–35.

who lived in cities outside of Roman Palestine. My aim is not to be exhaustive or to provide a catalogue of deities and religious movements. Instead, I offer a general characterisation aimed at conveying something of the place and roles of religion in the lives of people. I want to emphasise how varied, prominent, pervasive and popular the practice of religion was, probably for most people. For early Gentile Christians to disdain and renounce the religious practices of their pre-conversion lives meant to turn away from colourful and engaging cultic customs that offered a great deal to devotees. It also meant abandoning a central feature of common life in Roman cities and a major component in the things that united families and peoples. We cannot appreciate early Christian worship unless we keep before our eyes the fact that for Gentile Christians it represented a *replacement cultus*. It was at one and the same time both a religious commitment and a renunciation, a stark and demanding devotional stance with profound repercussions.

In chapter two I move on to an attempt to describe some general features of early Christian worship. Here my concern is to address the question of what devotees seem to have derived from their corporate devotional practice. They were expected to give up the rich religious 'pagan'[3] fare on offer in the Roman world. What did they derive from their Christian worship, which was to be their sole legitimate worship? Here we look at the setting and practices of first-century Christian worship, and the ways that Christians attributed large and powerful significance to their worship. We shall see that for early Christians their Christian worship gatherings provided alternative opportunities for shared religious experiences and the communal identity that they had formerly found in their

---

[3] The term 'pagan' has various connotations in various circles, including a derogatory one in some popular usage (i.e., depraved, etc.). I intend no such connotation here. Some New Testament scholars prefer to avoid the term altogether, but I know of no handy substitute. Moreover, the term is used among classicists and ancient historians simply to designate non- or pre-Christian and non-Jewish religions. This is how I intend the term in this book.

pagan religious practices. Also, we shall see how early Christian worship was endowed with rich meaning, even with transcendent significance, though it would have been seen outwardly as rather unimpressive in comparison with the often elaborate and striking ceremonies of the Roman environment.

Then, in chapter three, I turn to a rather detailed discussion of the place of Christ in the monotheistic worship of early Christians. Here I return to, and expand upon, an earlier itemised analysis of the cultic actions directed toward Christ and the way that Christ figures in the Christians' public and corporate devotional life.[4] Both in an earlier book and in this chapter, I aim to demonstrate that Christ was given the sorts of devotion that we can properly understand as full cultic worship, and that we can rightly describe Christian worship of the earliest observable decades as genuinely 'binitarian'. That is, I contend that at this surprisingly early stage Christian worship has two recipients, God and Christ, yet the early Christians understand themselves as monotheists and see their inclusion of Christ in their devotional life as in no way compromising the uniqueness of the one God to whom they had been converted through the gospel. This topic has been the subject of a good deal of investigation and debate in recent years, and so I engage a number of other scholars in this chapter, especially in the many notes.

These three chapters of historical investigation are followed by a final chapter directed toward questions about contemporary Christian worship. The discussion and views in the first three chapters do not presuppose any particular faith standpoint and will, I hope, be of some value to anyone with a historical interest in early Christianity. In this final chapter I write as a worshipping Christian, drawing upon scholarly research and offering some reflections intended to help shape Christian worship today. Those readers who have no personal interest in the contemporary practice of Christian faith are free to ignore the final chapter, of course. But I invite those who for any reason do not share Christian faith but who may find it

---

[4] L. W. Hurtado, *One God, One Lord: Early Christian Devotion and Ancient Jewish Monotheism.*

interesting to 'listen in' on one Christian addressing others about worship to consider this discussion as well as the historically oriented discussion in the first three chapters. I have neither the competence nor the space in this book to attempt anything but reflections on a selection of points that have to do with how Christians might regard their worship today and seek to inform it by the emphases and character of Christian worship in its foundational period.

Chapter 1

The Religious Environment

Early Christian worship did not take place in a religious vacuum. The Roman world was chock-full of religiosity, with a dizzying array of religious groups, movements, customs, activities and related paraphernalia. Earliest Christian faith did not represent religiousness over against irreligious culture, but had to enter the 'traffic' as a new movement on a very crowded and well-travelled highway of religious activity. This vibrant and diverse religious environment of the Roman world is very significant for understanding that world and for any accurate appreciation of earliest Christian worship.

If sound historical method involves attempting, insofar as possible, to view a subject of investigation in its historical context, then earliest Christian worship and devotional life must be seen within the context of religious features of the Roman world, especially the phenomena that have to do with the devotional life of the Roman period. Within the limits of this chapter it is not possible to discuss, or even to mention, the full range of matters that made up the religious environment of the time. Instead, I shall select a number of features of Roman-era religiousness that I hope will be of particular help in becoming acquainted with the setting in which Christian worship first appeared.[1] In later chapters we shall look more closely at the phenomena of earliest Christian worship and what the earliest Christians seem to have meant by and

---

[1] For brief descriptions of the Greek and Latin terms for religiousness, piety, etc., see 'Religion, Terms Relating to,' in Hammond and Scullard, *The Oxford Classical Dictionary*, 917.

derived from their devotional practices. Here, however, the aim is to prepare ourselves to see how Christian devotional practices were reflective of their period and setting, and perhaps also unusual or even deliberately counter to the dominant religiousness.

In what follows I am heavily dependent upon more detailed studies of the Roman religious environment by other scholars.[2] My own contribution in this chapter is limited to highlighting selected features of that environment as particularly important for a historical appreciation of earliest Christian devotional life and practice.

Though Jewish religious life of that era is certainly to be seen as part of the larger Roman environment, devout Jews saw their religious commitments and traditions as distinctive and characteristically held themselves aloof from much of the religious life of the larger Roman world. Consequently, I shall discuss Jewish religious life separately, after commenting on features of the 'pagan' or wider religious environment.

Ubiquity

Perhaps the first thing to emphasise is the pervasiveness of religion in the Roman world. It is in fact difficult to point to any aspect of life in that period that was not explicitly

---

[2] E.g. Ferguson, *Backgrounds of Early Christianity*, 112–253 (on the 'pagan' religious setting); 315–463 (on the Jewish religious background), gives both wide-ranging introductory discussion and bibliographical references. Finegan, *Myth & Mystery: An Introduction to the Pagan Religions of the Biblical World* surveys a wide range of religious traditions relative to the Old Testament and the New Testament periods. See also MacMullen, *Paganism in the Roman Empire*; Teixidor, *The Pagan God*; L. H. Martin, *Hellenistic Religions: An Introduction*; R. M. Grant, *Gods and the One God*; Armstrong (ed.), *Classical Mediterranean Spirituality: Egyptian, Greek, Roman*; Klauck, *Die religiöse Umwelt*. On women's religious life, often ignored in treatments of Roman era religion, see Kraemer, *Maenads, Martyrs, Matrons, Monastics: A Sourcebook on Women's Religions in the Greco-Roman World*.

connected with religion. Birth, death, marriage, the domestic sphere, civil and wider political life, work, the military, socialising, entertainment, arts, music – all were imbued with religious significance and associations. Any civic and public office also had religious connotations and often involved *ex officio* religious duties, such as public leadership in periodic ceremonies in honour of the city deities. Any association of tradesmen had its patron deity, and meetings included ritual gestures in honour of the deity. Practically any meal, and certainly any formal dinner, included ritual acknowledgement of deities, and might well be held in rooms that formed part of the temple of this or that deity. Each military unit had its patron deities and performed regular religious acts in honour of them. Divinities of the kitchen were acknowledged in daily home routines of cooking. So, in things grand and imposing, and in things routine and familiar, religion was involved and divinities revered as appropriate in various devotional actions.

To be sure, as there are now, there were also sceptics of religion then, some of whom were among the cultured elite, the *literati* whose works survive and who are characteristically among the sort of ancient writers studied in the Classics departments of universities. Among self-appointed sophisticates, then as now, it may even be that scepticism toward the validity and efficacy of religion was not infrequent. But all indications are that the overwhelming masses of people of the Roman period approvingly encountered religion everywhere and participated in religious activities both regularly and with enthusiasm.[3] Especially for those of us living in more secularised societies in which religion and religious institutions have been relegated to being one of many private pastimes and are

---

[3] Saffrey, 'The Piety and Prayers of Ordinary Men and Women in Late Antiquity,' in A. H. Armstrong (ed.), *Classical Mediterranean Spirituality*, 195–213. The over-reliance upon the literary works of classical authors to portray the attitudes and beliefs of ordinary people of the wider Roman world (all too common in some earlier periods of scholarship) would be like taking Gore Vidal as representative of late twentieth-century religious attitudes and practices.

seen as playing a very limited role in the larger society, it is important to try to realise the very prominent and ubiquitous place of religion in the Roman world.

Moreover, though scholars have sometimes made assertions about a loss of confidence in the gods in Roman paganism, these assertions seem to be either motivated by apologetic concerns (assuming and asserting the obvious superiority of Christianity) or based on simplistic historical assumptions (Christian faith caught on, so the religious competition must have been weak). The available evidence of Roman pagan religiosity indicates lively participation, and the many tangible expressions of thanks to the gods for answered prayers and various favours (e.g., the many *ex voto* artefacts that reflect popular religiosity) reflect a widely shared sense that the gods were active and that devotion to them 'worked' in bringing blessings of various types.[4]

Salience

Another way to appreciate the prominence and pervasiveness of religion in the Roman period is to note its sheer visibility. Major portions of city space were taken up with numerous temples, and these buildings were often the largest, most elaborate and expensive to be found in urban areas. One could not visit any Roman-era city without being struck forcibly by the place of the gods. The surviving architecture of the ancient world still reflects this, as any visitor to the Acropolis of Athens or the Forum in Rome can attest. These structures were made of expensive stone, were usually colourfully painted and decorated, and were situated prominently on central sites in the cities. Moreover, the building of new temple structures and the refurbishing and extension of existing ones were frequent throughout the Roman period. Visitors to practically any busy Roman-era city would likely have noted numerous

---

[4] See 'Votive Offerings' in Hammond and Scullard, *Oxford Classical Dictionary*, 1132–33.

construction projects, many concerned with religious structures.[5]

There were also shrines outside of cities. These shrines were sites of traditional devotion to the deities or places where more recent devotees had felt themselves instructed by a god or goddess to erect a shrine. Some of these shrines were large and very impressive and appear to have drawn large numbers of pilgrims to the special festivals and holy days associated with the deities honoured at the sites.

The ceremonies expressive of religious devotion were likewise highly visible. Indeed, they seem to have been intended to draw attention. Many deities had periodic (usually annual) ceremonies that included street processions involving choirs accompanied by various musicians, priests and other devotees specially attired, images of the deities paraded through the streets, and dramatic rituals, all of which drew crowds to watch and participate in the activities. These festivities sometimes also included elaborate performances by mimes and other players who acted out the myths associated with the deities. We have a description of such a procession in the classic entertaining (sometimes ribald) tale *The Golden Ass* by the second-century CE writer, Apuleius.[6] The author describes in some detail a procession in honour of Isis that includes people in various costumes representing different occupations and social roles; animals, some attired in human clothing; women and men in ceremonial dress; musicians; male and female initiates of the goddess; priests carrying cultic implements and symbols; and other individuals and statues representing various other deities.

Some of the temples had theatres attached to them where it is likely the traditional stories of the deities were acted out, probably on the major festival occasions associated with the deities in question. Feasting likewise was often a feature of

---

[5] L. M. White, *Building God's House in the Roman World: Architectural Adaptation among Pagans, Jews, and Christians*, 27–31.
[6] See, e.g., Graves (trans.), *The Transformations of Lucius, otherwise known as the Golden Ass by Lucius Apuleius*, 230–33.

these periodic celebrations, with wealthy patrons paying the costs.

For at least some deities, there were also daily rituals, such as those attested for Isis, which involved the ritual opening of her temples in the morning and their closing at the end of the day, and public bathing and dressing of the image of the goddess, all of this in elaborate gestures and often accompanied by music and singing. Given the large number of deities honoured in the Roman era, each with his or her own occasions and ceremonies, one could witness very public and striking religious ceremonies on any day of the week, and larger and more elaborate events at various times of the year.

In the Roman era religion was not only a private affair but was also seen as very much a public aspect of life. Religious ceremony was deliberately intended to be noticed and to engage the entire village or city. In fact, it is likely that the overwhelming number of all public events were explicitly religious in character, and the overwhelming majority of religious events and actions were public and expressive of one's participation in one's family, one's city and people, and in the larger Roman *oikoumene* (the Greek word for the Roman 'world' or 'empire').

Diversity

Along with the ubiquity and salience of religion in the Roman period, we must reckon with its diversity. For all people of that period, with the exception of devout Jews and then Christians, the gods were many and what we may call 'the divine' was manifested in many forms, with many divine beings, all of them in principle valid. Proper piety involved a willingness to honour all these manifestations of divinity according to the religious traditions associated with them. Save for the Jews, each ethnic group in the Roman world had its own assortment of deities to be reverenced. Some deities were particularly linked with this or that city (e.g., Athena with Athens, or Artemis with Ephesus) and were revered as protectors of their cities, the welfare of the cities being connected with proper reverence for the city deities.

It is also important to understand that having one's own traditional deities in no way prevented one from acknowledging the validity of the deities of other peoples. It was fully accepted that each ethnic group should have and continue to reverence their own deities. Official Roman imperial policy was to recognise and even to support the traditional religious devotion of all subject peoples. Local and touring Roman officials demonstrated this by visiting important shrines and making offerings in honour of their deities. This Roman policy even extended to Jewish religion, with its refusal to reverence other gods and its polemic against other religious traditions as idolatry.

In the Roman *oikoumene*, as people travelled about freely, relocated voluntarily to conduct business and trade, or were forcibly relocated through conquest and enslavement (often some time thereafter being made freedmen and freedwomen), the gods and religious practices of various peoples were set alongside one another, especially in the larger cities. Immigrants, and even slaves, were characteristically allowed to follow their ethnic religious traditions. When they were economically able to do so, they built shrines and temples to their own traditional deities in the cities and areas where they relocated. Thus, for example, Egyptian émigrés built shrines to Isis; Diaspora Jews built synagogues.

The very visible manner in which religion was characteristically conducted meant that the religious diversity and complexity of Roman cities was very salient as well. As one developed personal contacts with people of various backgrounds, one might have opportunities and invitations to participate in formal worship and less formal devotional practices directed to divinities other than those of one's own ethnic tradition. Such opportunities were usually welcomed and enjoyed, without any worry that by doing so one was in any way being untrue to one's own religious obligations or challenging the validity and claims of the traditional deities of one's own people. Visitors freely participated in the religious festivities of cities and areas they were in without any qualms of conscience.

It is in light of this open attitude and interested curiosity in the rich variety of religious traditions and practices on offer in Roman cities that we can understand the phenomenon of Gentiles frequenting Diaspora synagogues, as mentioned in the Acts accounts of Paul's travels, and Cornelius-type figures who even took some considerable interest in Jewish religion.[7] The many opportunities and invitations to participate in various religious activities afforded in Roman-era cities are also reflected in Paul's detailed instructions in 1 Corinthians 8–10, answering questions about Christians participating in the worship of other gods (10:1–22), accepting invitations to pagan temples with non-Christian acquaintances or family to share in religious feasts (8:7–13), and dining with non-Christians in other circumstances (10:27–30). Though Paul offers conditional acceptance of Christians dining with non-believers, he rejects outright any Christian participation in pagan worship, and even warns believers against any meal where the food is explicitly identified as being a sacrificial offering to a god. In his guardedness, Paul shows how much his stance is at odds with the dominant affirmation of religious diversity and the consequent freedom to participate in various cultic occasions that characterised the Roman period.

In addition to the variety of deities reflecting the various cities, peoples and regions of the Roman *oikoumene*, there was always the diversity of divine beings and associated devotional practices that pertained to various spheres of life, as mentioned earlier. At meals there might be small libations to the household gods, reverenced also with household shrines before which frequent devotion would be offered by the family. Regional or city deities were reverenced by the populace, especially in periodic festivals manifesting loyalty to the deities

---

[7] E.g., note references to Gentiles in Jewish synagogues in Acts 13:16, 48; 14:1; 17:1–5, 12; 18:4, and the description of Cornelius in Acts 10:1–5. On the evidence of Gentile proselytes and 'godfearers', see Levinskaya, *The Book of Acts in its Diaspora Setting*, 1–126.

and requesting their further good favour. The deities of one's guild were reverenced in meetings and at guild dinners. From the rule of Julius Caesar onward, initially in the East and then creeping through the West, the goddess Roma (representing imperial Rome itself) and the emperor too received all the gestures of devotion of ancient religion (temples, their images reverenced, sacrifices, hymns), expressing loyalty to Rome and genuine gratitude for the benefits of Roman rule.[8]

In addition to the very public cults, there were also a good many voluntary or private groups, sometimes devoted to a deity also worshipped in more official and public ways, and sometimes devoted to other gods than those of the more 'official' public religion of the city or area. These private cults often met in the homes of more well-off members and group dining seems to have been a frequent and central expression of their religious identity. Indeed, sometimes the members seem to have been largely or entirely made up of the extended household (including, of course, slaves) of a wealthy individual who was the leader of the group (interestingly, sometimes this leader was a wealthy woman).[9]

The Roman era was also characterised by a trans-local, even international dissemination of devotion to some divinities who, though often originating as local deities or deified heroes, acquired a much wider reputation and following. One of the most frequently cited of these is Isis, originally an Egyptian goddess of modest significance who was rather successfully promoted as goddess of the whole *oikoumene*.[10] In the case of Isis, we see an interesting demonstration of the full acceptance of diversity in religious traditions, as she came to be touted as the goddess reverenced by various peoples under

---

[8] L. R. Taylor, *The Divinity of the Roman Emperor*; Price, *Rituals and Power: The Roman Imperial Cult in Asia Minor*.

[9] L. M. White, *Building God's House*, 26–59.

[10] Egan, 'Isis: Goddess of the *Oikoumene*,' in L. W. Hurtado (ed.), *Goddesses in Religions and Modern Debate*, 123–42; Ferguson, *Backgrounds of Early Christianity*, 211–20. Hegedus attempts analysis of the geographical spread of the Isis cult across the Roman period.

many different names.[11] Often overlooked as another prime example of trans-local and trans-national dissemination of a particular religious tradition is the god of the Jews, who remained explicitly linked with the Jews but seems to have drawn varying degrees of interest from numerous Gentiles as well in cities such as Rome, Antioch, Alexandria and others where the Jewish Diaspora was concentrated.[12] As the deities and traditions of various peoples came into living contact with one another and were spread about, whether through conquest, trade, immigration, or other means, people found themselves with opportunities to take up devotion to deities that were new to them. We may thus speak of a growth of voluntary religious association in the Roman period.[13]

There have sometimes been references to the Roman era as a period of massive propagation of 'oriental' cults and of significant conversion of people to these new religious imports from Egypt, Syria and places further east. Two important caveats must be registered.[14] For one thing, the actual evidence of any significant appropriation of new religious traditions imported from one area to another is very slight. It appears that there were some limited successes for some very few deities exported beyond their home turf. In some cases they may have been seen as exotic, and thus attracted the attention of some with time and inclination to diversify their religious diet. These people were likely the better off, whose interest in 'foreign' gods drew the attention (and sometimes the complaints) of the literary elite, through whose writings we hear of such things. In the

---

[11] A frequently cited text is Apuleius, *The Golden Ass*, which in book 11 contains a prayer addressed to Isis that links her to various goddess figures (e.g., Ceres, Venus, Proserpine). For translation, see Graves, *The Transformations of Lucius*, 226–27.

[12] E.g., Levinskaya, *The Book of Acts*, 19–126.

[13] Kloppenborg and Wilson (eds.). *Voluntary Associations in the Graeco-Roman World*.

[14] The classic study is Nock, *Conversion: The Old and the New in Religion from Alexander the Great to Augustine of Hippo*. More recently, note MacMullen's trenchant analysis in *Paganism*, 94–112. Also relevant for my discussion is Teixidor, *The Pagan God*, esp. pp. 4–5, 144.

main, however, the devotees of the deities imported from the East appear in fact to have been immigrants (including slaves) who brought the gods with them from their native lands, plus of course their descendants, and often those they married.[15] Mithraism as we know it from Roman sites and sources is not evidenced at all in the eastern areas where it was once supposed to have originated, and seems more likely to have been a Roman innovation, probably in the West. Although of some popularity among military and low to middle-ranking governmental workers, it was never really propagated among the general populace.[16]

Secondly, even if one became a devotee of Isis or another such imported divinity, this was never understood as involving a neglect, much less any renunciation, of one's previous and other religious devotion, such as one's ancestral traditions or the deities of one's locale or city. That is, any spread of new deities in the Roman period did not really involve a 'conversion' from previous religious practices to new and exclusive religious commitments. Interest in imported deities and cults was ordinarily simply an additional, voluntary religious avocation added onto one's previous and wider religious activities and practices. This helps further explain why Paul found it necessary to deal with questions about whether Gentile Christians could continue to participate in pagan cults and frequent events in their honour. The exclusivism expected of Christian converts, a renunciation of all other cultic activities directed to any other gods, was paralleled only by the demands made on proselytes to Jewish religion. In this both Jewish and Christian demands were at odds with all other religious attitudes of the Roman era.

---

[15] E.g., the inscriptional evidence on devotees to Isis in Italy and Sicily referred to in MacMullen, *Paganism*, 14–15.

[16] Ulansey, *The Origins of the Mithraic Mysteries*, and *id.*, 'Solving the Mithraic Mysteries', *Biblical Archaeology Review* 20 (Sept/Oct 1994), 41–53; Beck 'Mithraism since Franz Cumont,' in Temporini and Haase (eds.), *Aufstieg und Niedergang der römischen Welt*, pp. 2003–2115.

The evidence indicates that although deities and religious traditions and practices sometimes underwent developments and changes, and although certain deities seem to have been more favoured in this time or that, in this area or that, and among this or that group of people, in general pagan religion did not undergo major changes. This is particularly so among the general populace, as reflected in inscriptional evidence and other archaeological data. We have no indication of a widespread decline in religious enthusiasm for the gods and the devotional practices concerned with them, no sense of a general religious malaise or dissatisfaction with traditional religion. The claims to the contrary, along with broad references to pagan 'anxiety' sometimes asserted as explanation for the success of early Christianity, have scant basis.[17]

Likewise with scant basis are the occasional scholarly assertions of a 'trend' or 'tendency' toward monotheism in the Roman period. To be sure, among some sophisticated writers in the ancient world there were attempts to posit a unity behind the diversity of gods. But this is hardly monotheism as we know it in classical forms of Judaism, Christianity or Islam, in which one deity is worshipped to the exclusion of all others. The pagan writers in question continued to affirm the validity of all the gods and the worship of them. They tended to see the gods as expressions and forms of some common divine essence that unified them all, and advocated the worship of the gods as proper reverence for all these valid manifestations of that divine essence. In short, the few expressions of a supposed monotheism never functioned as the basis for any significant change in religious practice, any challenge to the 'polytheistic' traditions and devotion of the time. We should really understand these assertions of a divine unity as attempts to find some abstract coherence in the diversity of gods and religious traditions that became so obvious in the Roman empire as many peoples and their traditions came into contact with one another. But there is no visible

---

[17] Teixidor, *The Pagan God*, 4–5, and MacMullen's more lengthy critique of Cumont and others in *Paganism*, 112–30.

difference in the religious practices of any of those who affirmed a divine unity of the gods.[18]

Sacred Places

As in nearly all times and cultures, in the Roman world, too, the practice of religion was particularly associated with sacred places. Though appeals to the gods might be made wherever the need arose, it was usually thought that there was special efficacy in approaching them in the temples, shrines and other sacred places with which they were more directly associated. Sacrifice in particular was more often than not deemed more appropriate in the sacred places, and in some cases sacrifice was forbidden elsewhere. So far as we know, for most devout Jews, for example, the Jerusalem temple was the only spot where blood sacrifice could legitimately be offered to the God of Israel. The other deities of the Roman era likewise characteristically had temples and shrines in their honour, and it would have been thought strange for a deity not to have any such sacred place.

In some cases, these sacred places were where tradition held that this or that deity had appeared to a devotee, the theophany making the location thereafter sacred to the honour of the divinity. Sometimes such theophanies were recounted as involving instructions from the deity to hallow the spot, perhaps even to erect a shrine. As I have already mentioned, in the case of the deities of cities, the temples were located on central and prominent sites, expressive of the central importance of the deities in the cities that particularly revered them as their protectors and providers of prosperity and well-being.

When cities or districts sought to express their devotion to the Roman emperor, they often sought his permission to erect a temple dedicated to him, or to place an image of the emperor alongside the image of the goddess Roma in the temples erected

---

[18] See references to modern scholarly claims of pagan 'monotheism' and my comments in *One God, One Lord: Early Christian Devotion and Ancient Jewish Monotheism*, 129–30.

to her, thereby making the temple a holy place for both Roma and the divine emperor. In this sort of action we have a clear demonstration of the sense that divinities are to be accorded sacred places where full worship of them can be carried out.

I have already mentioned the considerable amount of Roman-era civic space taken up by temples and the enormous expense they represented. We must remember that in any city of the time there were numerous temples and shrines dedicated to various deities. As, for example, MacMullan has noted with reference to cities in Italy:

> The standard Roman city . . . would need room for temples to the Capitoline Triad (Jupiter, Juno, and Minerva), plus Mercury, Isis and Sarapis, Apollo, Liber Pater, Hercules, Mars, Venus, Vulcan, and Ceres.[19]

These city temples were likely at least as common and as prominent as the many grand church buildings that dominated European cities until the recent prominence of office and financial towers on many city skylines.

In many cases, these monumental temples were complexes that included various facilities and served a variety of needs. I cite MacMullan again:

> To complete the picture of religious centres constituting also cultural centers, with zoological parks, aviaries, museums, concerts, art galleries, and public lectures, or the equivalent of all these things provided nowhere else in most cities, we must add botanical gardens . . .[20]

This means that the sacred places of the gods were not only prominent but heavily frequented, both for what we would think of as obviously religious purposes and for wider social and cultural purposes as well. In particular, cult centres were places where groups of people could eat and drink together

---

[19] MacMullen, *Paganism*, 1.
[20] Ibid., 35. The whole of MacMullen's discussion in *Paganism*, 34–42, offers valuable insight into Roman-era sacred places and their importance in the religious and cultural life of the time.

easily. I will say more about religious meals later in this discussion. At this point, however, I want to note that the temples of the pagan gods were also frequently used as convenient places for social dining and often had rooms attached to the central shrine that could be used (likely rented out) for such purposes.[21] Thus, part of the reason that Roman-era temples are to be seen as so important a feature of city life is that people frequented them for a range of purposes and combined social and religious life and activities easily within their precincts. A great deal of financial outlay was involved in shrines and temples, and a great deal of life was related to them.

Images

Just as characteristic as temples and shrines were cult images of the gods, the temples normally serving as houses of the gods as represented by their cult images. Here again we see the strongly visual nature of the religious environment of the Roman era. It was thought the most natural thing to have and use images representing the gods as foci of worship. As mentioned earlier, the emerging divine-emperor devotion of the early imperial period is particularly valuable to us in illustrating the importance of cult images. The requests from this or that city or region for the emperor's permission to honour him cultically included requests for permission to set up the emperor's image and give it cultic honours.[22] It was simply unimaginable to reverence any

---

[21] As MacMullen notes (*Paganism*, 36), even in larger houses of the Roman period it would have been difficult to accommodate a dining party larger than ten or so, and the living quarters of most people had no dedicated dining room at all. The temples afforded rooms and tables where friends and families, guilds and other groups could enjoy meals together. See also the discussion and drawings of temple structures showing such dining rooms, in Murphy-O'Connor, *St. Paul's Corinth: Texts and Archaeology*, 161–67.

[22] On emperor devotion, in addition to the works by Taylor and Price cited earlier, see Schowalter, *The Emperor and the Gods*. For further bibliography, see Herz, 'Bibliographie zum römischen Kaiserkult' in Temporini and Haase (eds.) *Aufstieg und Niedergang*.

figure as divine without registering this reverence in fashioning and using sacred images.

From the Jewish tradition of the time, early Christians inherited a prohibition against cult images. For this reason as well as others, their worship seemed strange to everyone else in the Roman world. Philosophers might discuss how the gods were not confined in the images and were really to be thought of as spiritual substances, with the images being poor material objects not to be confused with them. But these sophisticates did not advocate the abandonment of temples and their cult images; indeed, they thoroughly affirmed them, offering only a refined understanding of the metaphysical relationship between images and the deities they represented. They argued that the images merely functioned as objects to facilitate devotion to the gods, providing a localised and tangible focus for worship.[23]

We should not, however, conclude that this Jewish and Christian prohibition against cult images meant an absolute ban against any imagery in places of worship. From the Dura Europos excavations onward, we have acquired increasing evidence of the rich use of imagery in ancient Jewish synagogues, including the direct representation of biblical characters and symbols that likely referred to God (e.g., solar images).[24] The earliest surviving Christian art is from the third or perhaps late second century and includes representations of Jesus; but it appears that these did not function in the way cult images of the gods functioned in the general religious

---

[23] Bevan, *Holy Images: An Inquiry into Idolatry and Image-Worship in Ancient Paganism and in Christianity*. For Roman-era Jewish attitudes toward the cult images of the Gentiles, see, e.g., Philo, *Decal.* 66–76; *Wis.Sol.* 13–14.

[24] Hopkins, *The Discovery of Dura Europos*; Bickerman, 'Symbolism in the Dura Synagogue' in Bickerman, *Studies in Jewish and Christian History*; Hachlili, *Ancient Jewish Art and Archaeology in the Land of Israel*, and *id.*, 'Early Jewish Art and Architecture' in Freedman, D.N. (ed.), *Anchor Bible Dictionary*; Ovadiah 'The Art of the Ancient Synagogues in Israel' in Urman and Flesher, (eds.), *Ancient Synagogues: Historical Analysis and Archaeological Discovery*.

environment. That is, the earliest Christian images do not appear to have served as objects to which worship was directed.[25] This Jewish and Christian lack of cult images, along with their refusal to honour the images of the other gods, was a major reason for the charge against them of 'atheism'. The ubiquitous use of cult images in Roman-era religion makes the scruples against them among Jews and Christians, even in the Jerusalem temple, very significantly at odds with a major characteristic of the religious environment.

In the light of the important role and significance of cult images, we may better appreciate the significance of the honorific references to Christ as the image (*eikon*) of God (e.g., 2 Cor. 4:4; Col. 1:15). In a culture in which images of the gods served as their manifestations, and reverence shown to the images was regarded as reverence for the gods themselves, to regard Christ as the image of the true and living God surely connoted a high regard for him and possibly expressed an implied polemic against the cultic images of the religious environment. References to Christ as God's image are also a reflection of the cultic devotion that was accorded Christ and understood at the same time as offered also to God 'the Father'.

Rituals

It is hard to imagine the practice of religion without some form of rituals, actions invested with specially sacred significance and particularly expressive of piety that become regularised for this or that religious group or tradition. In the Roman era, as in nearly all ancient religion, there was a rich variety of ritual actions for various occasions and for various deities.

Sacrifice was a common ritual component of the worship of most divinities, including, of course, the God of Israel. Given the semantic development of our word 'sacrifice', which has come to connote loss suffered for the sake of someone or

---

[25] On early Christian attitudes toward the use of church imagery, see Finney, *The Invisible God: The Earliest Christians on Art*.

something else, with the emphasis placed on the cost to the one(s) making the sacrifice, it is necessary to stress that in the ancient world to sacrifice was to make an offering, a gift to the gods, and had a very positive, even joyous, meaning.[26] In most cases, for example, sacrificial offerings by individuals seem to have been as thanks to a god for blessings given, often in answer to a prayer. Sacrifice on behalf of groups too (e.g., cities, families, other groups) were most often likewise joyous events, the offering given gladly to the god as thanks.

We must also note, of course, that in most types of animal sacrifices a feast was a component of the ritual, the sacrificial victim providing the main course. Indeed, for many of the general populace of Roman times, the only occasions for eating meat were sacrificial events when the better off would provide sacrifices sufficient for the larger circle of participants, whether family, guild or city populace.[27] A portion of the sacrificial victim was given to the god, that is, to the temple and its priests as well. As a measure of the enthusiasm for animal sacrifice, often the temples could not make use of these offerings and thus sold excess meat to vendors who retailed it in the marketplace to the general public. This produced anxieties among some believers in Corinth as to whether they could purchase and eat meat from the market, for it might well have originated as an offering to a pagan god. Paul's assurance in 1 Corinthians 10:25–26 that Christians could eat such meat in good conscience is directed to these anxieties.

Along with the lack of temples or cult images, the earliest Christians offered no sacrifices to their God, and in this as well seemed to their pagan neighbours an odd sort of religious group. Their lack of these important 'normal' components of religion is part of the reason why some outsiders regarded

---

[26] Yerkes *Sacrifice in Greek and Roman Religions and Early Judaism*; also 'Sacrifice,' in Hammond and Scullard, *Oxford Classical Dictionary*, 943–45; Anderson 'Sacrifice and Sacrificial Offerings (OT)' in Freedman, D.N. (ed.), *Anchor Bible Dictionary*.

[27] 'For most people, meat was a thing never eaten and wine to surfeit never drunk save as some religious setting permitted' (MacMullen, *Paganism*, 40).

Christian groups as more like philosophical associations than religious groups.[28] That they took over from Jewish synagogue practice the reading of (Old Testament) scriptures and Christian writings (e.g., Paul's epistles), as well as sermons and addresses on religious topics, as regular components of their worship meetings further added to this 'scholastic' impression.

Early Christians were not without ritual, of course. Like some other religious groups of the time, they had an initiation ritual, in their case baptism, and invested it with rich significance.[29] The initiation rituals of pagan religious groups varied but were often elaborate and colourful, and sometimes deliberately exotic. This is particularly so for the religious groups often referred to as 'mystery cults'.[30] The ceremonies might be held (or culminate) at night by torchlight, with priests in full garb, sacred objects brought forth to view, incense, music or orchestrated loud noises, sonorous phrases recited, and special gestures such as disrobing and reclothing the initiate. The immediate aim seems to have been to create an impressive and memorable experience for the initiates and for observers. Although there may have been some such rituals, or some components of them, that were reserved for initiates and members of the cult, we should not imagine that the so-called 'mystery cults' were quite as thoroughly secretive as has sometimes been thought. The Eleusinian mysteries, for example, were quite public. For these groups as well, one aim of their rituals was to attract crowds and thereby recruit devotees or at least promote the renown of their god.[31] As with other matters, the early Christian initiation rite would have seemed rather 'low tech,'

---

[28] Judge, 'The Early Christians as a Scholastic Community', *Journal of Religious History* 1 (1960/61), 4–15, 125–37.

[29] E.g., Cullmann, *Baptism in the New Testament*; Beasley-Murray, *Baptism in the New Testament*. On comparisons between Christian and pagan rituals, see Nock, *Early Gentile Christianity and its Hellenistic Background*, esp. 109–45; Wedderburn, *Baptism and Resurrection: Studies in Pauline Theology against its Graeco-Roman Background*.

[30] M. W. Meyer, *The Ancient Mysteries: A Sourcebook*, gives an introduction and an anthology of ancient texts in translation.

[31] MacMullen, *Paganism*, 23–24.

simple, and comparatively less impressive to pagan observers used to these more elaborate events. True, there were lots of other house-based cultic associations in the Roman period, small and without the trappings of the more public cultic events, and thus resembling in some ways the Christian groups.[32] But, unlike the Christian worship meetings, these private cultic associations were never intended to replace the many other cultic activities of the pagan religious environment of the time. It is the exclusivist posing of comparatively unadorned house-church worship sessions over against the colourful ritual life of this environment that makes Christianity apparently unique.

Meals

At various points I have referred to meals as an important component of Roman-era religion.[33] As indicated already, sacrifice regularly included a meal shared by the devotees, and it would appear that all known religious groups had sacred meals that provided a very meaningful, favoured expression of their shared piety. But we must understand that this meal-piety was not at all a solemn one. The occasions themselves were very festive and eating and drinking were engaged in with enthusiasm and in copious measure. Indeed, among the rules to be observed at the entrances to some pagan shrines is a warning not to vomit up one's wine within the sacred precincts – which suggests the sort of occasion involved![34]

Among these sacred feasts, there were those held in honour of city or local gods and open to large numbers of the population, those for initiates only, and those private dinners that might be open to guests but for which an invitation was necessary. I have mentioned earlier that, especially in cities,

---

[32] L. M. White, *Building God's House*, 31–40.
[33] D. E. Smith, 'Greco-Roman Meal Customs' and 'Greco-Roman Sacred Meals' in Freedman, D. N. (ed.), *Anchor Bible Dictionary*.
[34] MacMullen, *Paganism*, 12, and 146 n. 58.

people would have opportunities and direct invitations to participate in various religious groups, often through sharing a meal in honour of this or that god. Though most such invitations were probably conveyed orally, written examples survive from antiquity.[35] Some of the invitations are to attend dinners in rooms attached to the temple of the god and others specify the location as a private home (both types of settings usually accommodating groups of eight to a dozen people). It is agreed among scholars that in all cases the meals in question had a religious significance and character. Indeed, it appears that the god in whose honour the meal was held was understood as present at the table participating in some spiritual way in the meal, probably as its host or guest of honour.[36] In fact, in one surviving invitation, the god Sarapis himself extends the invitation![37] This conception that the gods were present at such meals likely lies behind Paul's warnings to Corinthian Christians that they are not to partake of the 'cup of demons' or participate in the 'table of demons' (1 Cor. 10:20–21), his pejorative references to feasts in honour of pagan gods.[38]

The best known Jewish sacred meal is, of course, the Passover feast.[39] This too was to be celebrated in a joyous mood, and it seems likely that, along with the singing of Psalms and the reclining posture required for the meal, the later rabbinic directive that the Passover must include four cups of wine preserves the festive nature of the occasion as celebrated in the

---

[35] Horsley, 'Invitations to the *kline* of Sarapis' in Horsley (ed.), *New Documents Illustrating Early Christianity*, 5–9, gives very good discussion with texts and translations.

[36] See discussion of texts and visual representations in Horsley, 'Invitations' 6, 8.

[37] One Oxyrhynchos text reads 'The god calls you to a banquet being held in the Thoereion tomorrow from the ninth hour.' Text and translation in Horsley, 'Invitations', 5.

[38] Paul's reference to being invited to dinners by unbelievers (εἴ τις καλεῖ ὑμᾶς τῶν ἀπίστων; 1 Cor. 10:27) echoes the wording of the written invitations, as noted by Horsley, 'Invitations', 9.

[39] Bokser, 'Unleavened Bread and Passover, Feasts of', in Freedman, D. N. (ed.), *Anchor Bible Dictionary*.

Second Temple period.[40] The Passover was properly celebrated in Jerusalem as long as the Jerusalem temple stood, but
there were other opportunities for devout Jews to express their
faith through a group meal (e.g., new moons) without having
to be in Jerusalem. The Qumran community had its own
shared meal endowed with special religious significance and
celebrated in a very joyous mood.[41] To be sure, it is likely that
Jewish sacred meals were less prone to excesses in drinking
and behaviour that seem to have been a feature of, or that had
to be more consciously warned against, in pagan feasts. But
with or without such excesses, the sacred meal of antiquity
was a joyous social occasion, and no tension was felt between
the religious character of the sacred meal and this social
dimension.

Given the ubiquitous role of meals in the religious environment of the time, it is understandable that in early Christian
circles a sacred meal was a characteristic feature of their collective devotional life. These meals of Christian fellowship
were held in the homes of believers with space to accommodate them (though, again, we should bear in mind that most
homes would not have been adequate for group dinners of
more than eight to ten people).

Jewish Religious Life

Though I have made a few short references to Jewish religion
in the preceding discussion, I wish now to make some more
extensive comments. Given the importance of Jewish religion
for the origins of Christianity, it is worth singling out this facet
of the Roman religious environment for special attention.
Again, I must be selective and will focus on certain features of

---

[40] See the recent review of various types of Jewish meals that have
been considered as context for the accounts of the Last Supper in the
gospels by Kodell, *The Eucharist in the New Testament*, 38–52.
[41] K. G. Kuhn, *Enderwartung und gegenwärtiges Heil:
Untersuchungen zu den Gemeindeliedern von Qumran*.

the practice of Jewish piety in the early Roman imperial period contemporary with the origins of Christianity.[42]

I have already mentioned two features of ancient Jewish religion that marked it off from the larger Roman religious environment: the absence of cult images and the exclusivity demanded. Both of these features were noted by pagan observers of the time. Neither in synagogues nor even in the Jerusalem temple where sacrifice was offered was there an image of the God of Israel serving like the cult images characteristic of Roman-era religion. Pagans often found this curious.

Jewish religious exclusivity was more than curious; it was considered downright antisocial behaviour. It would certainly have had profound, unavoidable effects upon the social interactions of devout Jews with non-Jews in Diaspora settings, given the ties of almost any social occasion to the gods. Some Jews simply assimilated to the pagan practice, and, no doubt, many others developed various degrees of compromise and accommodation. But both Jews and non-Jews knew quite well that faithfulness to Jewish religion involved deep scruples about participation in devotion to other gods.

In addition, there were strong scruples against inappropriate reverence for God's own heavenly retinue of angels or for other agents of God such as the revered patriarchs (e.g., Moses) or messiahs. Jewish 'monotheism' could take in quite a rich assortment of very exalted and powerful beings in addition to God, but cultic worship (that is, public corporate prayer and

---

[42] Though there are many studies on Jewish religion of the period, most focus mainly on the literature, beliefs, parties and institutions, and have little to say directly about the practice of Jewish piety. Among exceptions, see Sanders, *Judaism: Practice and Belief, 63 BCE–66 CE*; several chapters in Safrai and Stern, *The Jewish People in the First Century: Historical Geography, Political History, Social, Cultural and Religious Life and Institutions*; Schürer, *The History of the Jewish People in the Age of Jesus Christ*, 3/1:138–49. Nickelsburg and Stone, *Faith and Piety in Early Judaism: Texts and Documents*, is a helpful anthology and gives beliefs and some features of practice, but surprisingly little of the latter given the title of the book.

praise, and of course sacrifice) was characteristically restricted to God alone.[43]

There were two main institutions for collective expressions of Jewish religion in this period: the temple in Jerusalem and the synagogue. For most Jews the Jerusalem temple was recognised as the only legitimate place where sacrifice could be offered to God, and many thousands of Jews from elsewhere in Roman Palestine and from the Diaspora made pilgrimages to Jerusalem for one or more of the great festal occasions: Passover, First-Fruits (Pentecost), and Ingathering or Booths (*Sukkoth*).[44] Jews who could not make the journey to Jerusalem still participated in and supported the operation of the temple through the annual temple tax (the 'half-shekel' contribution required of all adult males, which was collected in various Diaspora cities and transported to Jerusalem).

But for most Jews the more familiar collective expression and exercise of religion was through their synagogues and families.[45] Especially in the Diaspora, where Jews were

---

[43] Hurtado, 'First-Century Jewish Monotheism', *Journal for the Study of the New Testament* 71 (1998), pp. 3–26.

[44] On the temple and its operation, see Sanders, *Judaism*, 47–118; Safrai, 'The Temple,' in Safrai and Stern, *The Jewish People*, 865–907; F. J. Murphy, *The Religious Word of Jesus: An Introduction to Second Temple Palestinian Judaism*, 71–92; Jeremias, *Jerusalem in the Time of Jesus*; Schürer, *History of the Jewish People*, 2: 237–313; Hayward, *The Jewish Temple: A Non-Biblical Sourcebook*. It appears that the Qumran sect considered the Jerusalem temple to have come under dubious priestly administration, with an incorrect religious calendar of sacred events and sacrifices of questionable validity. In this attitude they were unusual among devout Jews of the time. Jerusalem itself retained a special significance and the Qumran group hoped for an eschatological purging that would involve a new temple with valid sacrifices and a legitimate priestly leadership and calendrical system. See, e.g., Schiffman, *Reclaiming the Dead Sea Scrolls*, 262–68, 385–94.

[45] Schiffman, *Reclaiming the Dead Sea Scrolls*, 423–63; Safrai, 'The Synagogue,' in Safrai and Stern, *The Jewish People*, 908–44; Urman and Flesher, *Ancient Synagogues*.

minorities and Jewish religious identity would have been
under constant pressure to assimilate with the dominant religious culture, it is likely that synagogues played an important
role in maintaining some level of religious solidarity among
Jews.[46] Diaspora Jews were often granted special rights by the
Romans, which included the right to meet together and practice their ancestral religious customs.[47] Thus, the synagogue,
the principal expression of Jewish collective religious identity,
would have held strong ethnic, political, social and religious
meanings.

The word 'synagogue' derives from the Greek word
synagoge and means a 'gathering', but the earlier Greek term
used for the religious meeting places of Diaspora Jews is
proseuche, '[place of] prayer', indicating that worship of God
was a major purpose of the gatherings in these places. There
may have been some major differences in practice between
Palestinian and Diaspora synagogues, but here I am mainly
concerned with Diaspora settings, where the greater number
of early Christian groups (whether Jewish Christians or
Gentile Christians) would have encountered Jewish practice.

There was no standardised prayer book or synagogue
liturgy in the Second Temple period, no fixed prayers or standardised lectionary, but there were probably somewhat
conventionalised practices that had developed over time. After
all, by the first century, Jewish synagogues had been a feature
of Diaspora Jewish life in at least some centres for two hun-
dred years or more.[48] Thus, synagogue prayers in various
places may well have been characterised by a number of
widely echoed themes, such as those that subsequently became
standardised in the *Eighteen Benedictions*, which became the

---

[46] E.g., Kasher, 'Synagogues as "Houses of Prayer" and "Holy
Places" in the Jewish Communities of Hellenistic and Roman Egypt'
in Urman and Flesher (eds.), *Ancient Synagogues*.
[47] Josephus lists numerous Roman decrees granting or reaffirming
rights to Jews in various cities and districts in *Antiq.* 14:213–64.
[48] See, e.g., Griffiths, 'Egypt and the Rise of the Synagogue' in
Urman and Flesher (eds.), *Ancient Synagogues*, 3–16.

central prayer of the synagogue liturgy.[49] Thanksgiving to God
for his gifts and mercies, and petitions for his continued mercy
upon Israel were likely common. We get some idea of what
was considered devout praying in the prayers recorded in various Jewish texts written or used in the Second Temple period
(e.g., Dan. 9:4–19; *Tobit* 3:1–6, 11–15; *Judith* 9:2–14).[50]

The *Shema*, a confession of faith that begins with the
famous words, 'Here, O Israel, the Lord our God, the Lord is
One' and composed of Deuteronomy 6:4–9; 11:13–21 and
Numbers 15:37–41, was probably widely (universally?)
recited in synagogues.[51] This confession expressed the exclusivist monotheism of devout Jews of the time that we have
already noted and was thus a crucial liturgical marker of Jewish religious identity over against the larger religious diversity
of the Roman period.[52] The Nash Papyrus suggests
catechetical or liturgical use of the *Shema* in Egypt well before
the birth of Christianity.[53]

There was also likely to have been singing or chanting of
biblical Psalms and perhaps other Psalm-like compositions

---

[49] On the origins and development of Jewish synagogue liturgy, see
Elbogen, *Der jüdische Gottesdienst in seiner geschichtlichen
Entwicklung*; and now Reif, *Judaism and Hebrew Prayer: New
Perspectives on Jewish Liturgical History*. On earliest evidence of
synagogue prayer, see also Talmon, 'The Emergence of Institutionalised Prayer in Israel in the Light of the Qumran Literature' in Delcor
(ed.), *Qumran. Sa piété, sa théologie, et sa milieu*; Falk, 'Jewish
Prayer Literature and the Jerusalem Church in Acts' in Bauckham
(ed.), *The Book of Acts in its First Century Setting*. For an introduction to traditional Jewish prayer, see Kimelman, Reuven, 'The
Shema and the Amidah: Rabbinic Prayer' in Kiley (ed.), *Prayer from
Alexander to Constantine: A Critical Anthology*, 108–20.
[50] Enermalm-Ogawa, *Un langage de prière juif en grec: Le
temoinage des deux premieres livres des Maccabées*; N. B. Johnson,
Prayer in the Apocrypha and Pseudepigrapha.
[51] 'The *Shema*' and the *Shemoneh 'Esreh*', in Schürer, *History of the
Jewish People*, 2:454–63.
[52] Hurtado, 'Jewish Monotheism'.
[53] Albright, 'A Biblical Fragment from the Maccabean Age: The
Nash Papyrus'.

such as are attested in the Qumran materials (the hymn scroll and the extra-canonical psalms).[54] Especially on occasions celebrating new moons and annual festivals such as Hannukah, chanting or singing may have been a major feature of Jewish synagogue worship.

Most frequently attested, however, is the reading of scripture as the central activity expressing Jewish religious identity in synagogues. Though there was probably not a fixed lectionary system, it seems likely that synagogues made efforts to have the whole of the Torah (the Pentateuch) read through in weekly synagogue meetings over a few years. Readings from the Prophets were also likely in many synagogues of the time. Some sort of homily was probably frequent as well. The reading of scripture and homilies are reflected in, for example, the NT accounts of synagogue activities (e.g., Acts 13:15), which must be taken as evidence of first-century practice known to the authors.[55] Both Josephus and Philo of Alexandria attest scripture reading and explanation and teaching based on scripture as regular features of weekly synagogue meetings of the first century CE.[56] In Diaspora synagogues it is likely that the scriptures were read in Greek, the translation of the Hebrew Bible into Greek having begun in the third century BCE, largely, it appears, to meet the desire of Greek-speaking Jews to read and study their scriptures.[57] The reading of Jewish scriptures in the Greek vernacular would also have enabled Gentile visitors to Diaspora synagogues to follow things and

---

[54] Grózinger, *Musik und Gesang in der Theologie der frühen jüdischen Literatur*; Flusser, 'Psalms, Hymns and Prayers' in Stone (ed.), *Jewish Writings of the Second Temple Period*, 551–77; Charlesworth, 'Jewish Hymns, Odes, and Prayers (ca. 167 B.C.E.–135 C.E.)' in Kraft and Nickelsburg (eds.), *Early Judaism and its Modern Interpreters*.

[55] Perrot, 'The Reading of the Bible in the Ancient Synagogue' in Mulder and Sysling (eds.), *Mikra: Text, Translation, Reading and Interpretation of the Hebrew Bible in Ancient Judaism and Early Christianity*, 137–59.

[56] E.g., Josephus, *Contra Apion* 2:175; Philo, *De Somiis* 2:127.

[57] E.g., Tov, 'The Septuagint' in Mulder and Sysling (eds.) *Mikra*, 161–88.

to learn about Jewish religion. That is, for Diaspora Jews, the liturgical reading of their scriptures functioned in some sense also as a means of promoting knowledge of their religion, and offering a view of them as a people whose religious tradition valued reading and learning.

Like other religious groups of the era, Jews also had religious meals that served as important expressions of their faith. The weekly Sabbath (Friday) evening meal held a religious significance. As mentioned earlier, on special occasions such as New Moon and annual festivals (e.g., Unleavened Bread/Passover, Pentecost, Booths [*Sukkoth*], Dedication of the Temple) Jews held religious feasts that were more elaborate, with wine and the best food they could provide.[58] Like many other examples of common meals with religious character in the Roman period, these religious meals expressed group solidarity in the religion, memorialised great events in Jewish religious history, and were festive, celebratory affairs.

It is difficult to know more precisely how Jews thought of the sacred character of these meals and whether they were understood to have any sort of 'sacramental' sense, in the sense of God being present with them in some way in their religious feasts, as seems to have been thought by pagans. The Qumran sect certainly attached great importance to their community meals, and reports about Jewish groups called Essenes and Therapeutae claim that they held meals with strong religious significance. But scholars do not agree on (1) whether or how the Qumran community is related to the Essenes or the Therapeutae, and (2) whether Jewish festal meals or those of the Qumran sect are really to be understood as 'sacramental', that is, as somehow conveying a 'real presence' of God.[59]

---

[58] Schürer, *History of the Jewish People* 3/1: 144–45 for discussion and references to primary evidence.

[59] On the character of the Qumran meals, cf. Kuhn's essay, *Enderwartung und gegenwärtiges Heil*, cited earlier; Schiffman, *The Eschatological Community of the Dead Sea Scrolls*, 59–67. For citations of the ancient sources and discussion of the relationship of Qumran to these other groups, see, e.g., Schürer, *History of the Jewish People* 2: 583–97.

Sacrificial meals shared by worshippers in the Jerusalem temple would certainly have been seen as particularly significant, and Philo's reference to God as 'the Host . . . to Whom the material provided for the [sacrificial] feast has come to belong . . .'[60] suggests that the sacrificial feast involves some sort of relation between God and the devotees who eat the sacrificial food. It is quite possible that in various ways Diaspora Jews saw their special religious feasts as being more than simply memorial celebrations. But we should be careful about reading too many Christian eucharistic ideas back into Jewish religious meals. Perhaps, however, the eucharistic ideas reflected in the early Christian writing known as the *Didache*, which seems to bear strong traces of Jewish-Christian influences, may not be too far from the ways Jews saw their religious feasts: as ritual realisations of their religious solidarity and of God's merciful provisions and promises.[61]

In addition to the synagogue, the home was an important locus of religious life. Sabbath, the chief weekly religious festival, was celebrated in the home as well as in the synagogue, with the Friday evening meal being a regular occasion for shared family piety. Daily prayers (morning and evening), perhaps including recitation of the *Shema*, were offered by devout Jews in their own homes, and may well have been additional opportunities for families to express their religious devotion.[62] Among some pious Jews of the time, *tefillin* (leather devices for strapping key portions of the Bible to the arms and forehead for prayer) were used, as were *mezuzoth* (small containers to hold biblical passages, characteristically the *Shema*, attached to the doorways of homes). These implements of Jewish piety are mentioned in Diaspora sources[63] and Roman-era examples have been found at the Qumran

---

[60] *Spec.Leg.* 1:221.
[61] *Did.* 9–10. We shall examine early Christian eucharistic practices and ideas in the next chapter.
[62] Safrai, 'Religion in Everyday Life,' in Safrai, S. and Stern, M. (eds.), *The Jewish People*, 793–833.
[63] Arist. 158–60.

site, suggesting a certain degree of shared practice both in Roman Palestine and the Diaspora.[64]

Whether in the synagogue or in the home, whether in Roman Palestine or the Diaspora, prayer facing toward Jerusalem seems to have been a widely practised feature of Jewish piety. The earliest allusion to this practice is found in Daniel 6:10. Early synagogues were arranged to enable prayer to be said toward Jerusalem.[65] In this we have one of many indications of the religious importance of Jerusalem and its temple. This temple orientation also conveyed to devout Jews that, wherever they were and whatever their sense of local involvement, they were also part of a trans-local religious tradition with historic roots and strong collective ties.

Summing Up

Much more could be said about the religious environment of earliest Christianity, but I hope that I have succeeded in making some basic points, the most fundamental being the value of giving attention to the Roman religious environment for a historical understanding of early Christian devotional life and practice. As I have pointed out earlier, in some ways (e.g., house fellowship involving a sacred meal) their worship setting and practices can be seen as reflective of that environment. In other ways, especially in pagan converts forsaking all other deities and cults, they were very different. It is to be expected that Christians in the Roman era reflected in various ways their historical setting in their beliefs and religious practice, and also that in some features they may have been distinguishable; but only patient analysis of early Christian religiousness in its

---

[64] Josephus too alludes to both the *mezuzah* and *tefillin*, *Antiq.* 4:212–13.

[65] Landsberger, 'The Sacred Direction in Synagogue and Church', *Hebrew Union College Annual* 28 (1957), pp. 181–203; Erik Peterson, 'Die geschichtlichen Bedeutung der jüdischen Gebetsrichtung' in Peterson, *Frühkirche, Judentum und Gnosis: Studien und Untersuchungen*.

historical context can help us see accurately how and where either was the case.[66]

Second, as I have already stated, it is clear that the religious environment of earliest Christianity was diverse, vigorous and flourishing. It is not as though there were large portions of the population of the Roman empire who were religiously dissatisfied and waiting for something like Christianity to come along to provide them with religious meaning. It is a mistake, therefore, to try to explain the spread of Christian faith in the Roman empire as the success of a vigorous religious movement over against some sort of pervasive religious ennui. The fact that some pagans embraced Christian faith and renounced their former religious life, and that some Jews recognised in the Christian gospel an eschatological revelation of the God of Israel cannot be accounted for by attributing to Roman paganism or to Jewish religion of the era a failure to provide meaningful and reasonably effective means of carrying on a devotional life. Christianity had to compete in a very active religious 'market', and if it won adherents it did so by offering 'products' and 'services' that could be perceived as comparing favourably with what else was on offer. Particularly because, as was demanded of full proselytes to Jewish religion, Christians were expected to make their Christian faith their sole religion and renounce participation in the other religious options of the time, what was offered in Christian groups had to have been seen by adherents as worth forsaking the alternatives. Powerfully attractive features must have been perceived.[67] Moreover, Christianity should probably be seen as having had some success in helping to shape the 'market', in much the way entrepreneurs offering new products and

---

[66] MacMullen, Ramsey and Lane, *Paganism and Christianity 100–425 C.E.*, is an accessible collection of various evidence relevant to the approach I advocate, though it is concerned more with 'late antiquity,' and thus with the situation later than earliest Christian practice.

[67] For example, MacMullen has emphasised the importance of Christian claims to work miracles, at least in the second century and thereafter (Christianizing the Roman Empire, A.D. 100–400).

services often have to create or enhance a public perception that they are needed. For example, we must suppose that Paul's success in winning converts depended in part upon his first persuading them that their pagan religious devotion was misguided and that they were in need of redemption from their religious past.

However, it is not my purpose in this book to focus on why Christianity grew, but to characterise early Christian worship. My point here is that in their worship early Christians found themselves in a lively and active religious environment. In the chapters that follow, I wish to look at selected features of earliest Christian worship in the light of this religious environment, and give particular attention to the incorporation of Christ as the recipient of cultic devotion which gave Christian worship a distinctive 'binitarian' shape that distinguished it from pagan and Jewish practices of the time.

Chapter 2

Features of Early Christian Worship

There are basically two main identifying marks of early Christian worship, when considered in its religious context: (1) Christ is reverenced as divine along with God, and (2) worship of all other gods is rejected. We shall consider the first of these in the next chapter. Our discussion in this chapter takes as its premise the latter identifying mark, the exclusivity of earliest Christian worship, which Wayne Meeks has judged 'perhaps the strangest characteristic of Christianity, as of Judaism, in the eyes of the ordinary pagan.'[1]

From the Jewish tradition of the time, earliest Christianity inherited a monotheistic exclusivity of worship, demanding of adherents a renunciation of the worship of other gods. Christian Jews, at least for the first few decades of the Christian movement, appear to have continued their participation in synagogues and in temple-based religious activities and events in Jerusalem (e.g., annual feasts such as Passover, prayer in the temple, sacrifices).[2] Paul, the apostle to the Gentiles, continued determinedly his Jewish religious associations, most markedly demonstrated in his repeated willingness to undergo synagogue floggings, which were dispensed as punishments for unspecified violations of Jewish religiousness as judged by synagogue authorities (2 Cor. 11:24). That is, in the earliest

---

[1] Meeks, *The First Urban Christians: The Social World of the Apostle Paul*, 160. The whole of Meeks's chapter on early Christian 'ritual' (pp. 140–63) is very much worth consultation.

[2] For examples of Jerusalem temple participation, see, e.g., Acts 2:46; 3:1; 5:12, 21, 42; 21:17–26.

period at least, the exclusivity of Christian worship did not extend to a refusal to participate in Jewish worship. The obvious reason is that the God of the earliest Christians was understood to be the God of the Old Testament and Israel, the God worshipped in the synagogue and Jerusalem temple. But participation in pagan religious groups and activities was another matter altogether.

Though Paul permitted his Gentile converts in Corinth to continue socialising with their pagan neighbours under some conditions (1 Cor. 10:23–30), he rejected outright any participation in activities with any explicit or obvious reverence directed to the pagan gods (1 Cor. 8:1–13; 10:14–22, 28).[3] This meant foregoing many diverse religious activities outside of Christian worship. For example, Christians were not to join their neighbours in cultic events explicitly honouring other gods, such as sacrificial feasts and cult dinners. It would also have been highly questionable to participate in the colourful religious parades and other ceremonies honouring the city gods. In short, the spectrum or 'menu' of acceptable religious activities and devotion was severely restricted for Christians, especially the Gentile converts whose preconversion religiosity would have taken in as much as they wished to accommodate from the full range of religious devotion and deities on offer. In place of the varied 'diet' of pagan religious options and activities, for Christians there was to be worship directed only to the one God in the name of Jesus.

In addition, earliest Christianity had no sacred places, no shrines, no imposing temple structures, no cultic images of God or Christ to focus and stimulate devotion, no impressive public processions, no priesthood or sacrificial rites. All in all, in the context of the cultic expression of religion in the Roman era, earliest Christian worship would have seemed a fairly modest, even unimpressive affair. It was definitely 'low-tech'. In this light also, converts can be thought of as

---

[3] Borgen, ' "Yes," "No," "How Far?"': The Participation of Jews and Christians in Pagan Cults' in Engberg-Pedersen (ed.), *Paul in His Hellenistic Context*, also Winter, 'Acts and Roman Religion' in Gill and Gempf (eds.), *The Book of Acts in its Graeco-Roman Setting*.

having been asked to forfeit a lot from the larger religious environment that seems to have provided enjoyment and addressed various religious and social needs. Yet, converts and adherents to Christian groups there certainly were. We might approach early Christian worship, therefore, by seeking for features that both characterised it and might have constituted its appeal or value for Christian converts who were asked to forego so much else. We are not primarily interested here in features that were unique to Christian worship. Instead, we seek to understand what Christian worship of the first century offered to converts. I shall organise the following discussion by identifying some general features.

Intimacy

The physical setting of earliest Christian worship was the home, in most cases probably the homes of comparatively better-off Christians with sufficient economic resources to have space to accommodate worship gatherings.[4] More specifically, since the common meal was a central component of first-century Christian worship, the setting was likely the dining area of the home. Excavation of the homes of the prosperous in Roman cities shows that dining rooms could rarely accommodate groups of more than nine or so, when one allows for the couches on which diners reclined in the Hellenistic fashion that was so widely followed in the Roman period. Even if the atrium area of the home were used for additional dining space, most Roman villas could have accommodated a group no larger than forty to fifty.[5] So the domestic setting, the size of the house-church group, and the characteristic central place of a shared meal in the

---

[4] On the development of Christian places of worship, see L. M. White, *Building God's House in the Roman World: Architectural Adaptation among Pagans, Jews, and Christians*, also Blue, 'Acts and the House Church' in Gill and Gempf (eds.) *Acts*.

[5] Murphy-O'Connor, *St. Paul's Corinth: Texts and Archaeology*, 153–61.

worship practice can all be seen as likely contributing to a social intimacy and strong solidarity among participants.[6]

To judge from Paul's statement that, 'Because there is one bread, we who are many are one body, for we all partake of the one bread' (1 Cor. 10:17), it would appear that characteristically the Pauline house-church groups manifested their social intimacy ceremonially in sharing a loaf of bread as part of the common meal. In the gospels' accounts of the Last Supper, Jesus is pictured as breaking a loaf of bread and passing it to the disciples as well as passing around a cup of wine (e.g., Mark 14:22–23). If, as is commonly accepted, these narratives were intended both to prefigure and reflect the eucharistic practices of the early churches, the accounts of Jesus' actions may be additional evidence that the commonality and intimacy of the house-church gathering were expressed vividly in sharing both a single loaf and a common cup.

The solidarity and intimacy of early Christian groups at worship are also vividly reflected in what appears to have been another characteristic gesture, the kiss of Christian liturgical fellowship. There are references to the 'holy kiss' in several Pauline letters (Rom. 16:16; 1 Cor. 16:20; 2 Cor. 13:12; 1 Thess. 5:26) and probably the same gesture is referred to as the 'kiss of love' in 1 Peter 5:14. The simple exhortation to share the kiss, without any further explanation, indicates that the gesture was quite broadly practised and familiar among first-century Christian groups. Given that New Testament epistles seem to have been composed for liturgical reading and incorporate liturgical formulae (e.g., the 'grace and peace' salutation and grace-benediction, the 'amen' and 'Abba, Father' prayer expressions, the 'maranatha' of 1 Cor. 16:22), it is likely that the 'holy kiss' or 'kiss of love [*agape*]' is to be understood as given and received in the worship setting.[7] Later references to the holy kiss in

---

[6] See Meeks, *Urban Christians*. 157–62, on 'The Lord's Supper: Ritual of Solidarity'.

[7] On liturgical formulae in Paul's letters, see J. L. White, 'New Testament Epistolary Literature in the Framework of Ancient Epistolography' in Temporini and Haase (eds.) *Aufstieg und*

Christian writings of the second and subsequent centuries consistently treat it as a liturgical action, often linked specifically with the Eucharist.[8] Also, we learn that it was given mouth-to-mouth, an exchanged kiss, expressing mutual intimacy and affection among all congregants, and that, for the first century or so at least, the kiss was exchanged with members of one's own sex and the opposite sex as well. In time, from fears of impropriety and in efforts to abate pagan rumours of Christian promiscuity, later church authorities sought to restrict the kissing to members of one's own sex.[9] Similarly motivated were rules that the holy kiss was to be given with mouths closed and that no second kiss was permitted![10] New Testament warnings against adultery (e.g., 1 Thess. 4:1–8) likely reflect a recognition that inappropriate sexual interests could develop among Christians precisely because of the intimacy among them fostered in their worship practice and wider religious ethos.

For a number of ancient Mediterranean peoples, the kiss as a sign of greeting, respect and affection was a common gesture for members of the same family, and in Middle Eastern societies was extended to broader circles of social acquaintances to signal honour and fellowship (e.g., Jesus' rebuke of his dinner host for not greeting him with a kiss in Luke 7:45). But the early Christian practice seems somewhat unusual in making the kiss a regular liturgical gesture and in extending the circle of allowed intimacy to all congregants of both sexes.

---

[7] *(continued) Niedergang der römischen Welt*, esp. 1739–49; Wu, 'Liturgical Elements' in Hawthorne and Martin (eds.) *Dictionary of Paul and His Letters*.

[8] Brooks, 'Kiss of Peace' in Ferguson (ed.), *Encyclopedia of Early Christianity*, 521–22; Thraede, 'Ursprung und Formen des "hl. Kuss" in frühen Christentum', *Jahrbuch für Antike und Christentum* 11/12 (1968–69), 124–80; Stählin, 'Φιλεω' in Kittel and Friedrich (eds.), *Theological Dictionary of the New Testament*; Benko, *Pagan Rome and the Early Christians*, 79–102.

[9] E.g., *Apostolic Constitutions* 2.7; 8.2.10 (*ANF* 7.422, 486).

[10] Athenagoras, *Legatio* 32 (*ANF* 2.146).

The language of earliest Christian discourse used in collective worship is expressive of intimacy.[11] Christians referred to one another as brothers and sisters, children of the same heavenly Father, or members of one body (1 Cor. 12:27). It is likely that, as members of what social scientists might describe as a 'fictive family' of brothers and sisters in Christ, earliest Christians deemed the familiarity of the fellowship kiss, acceptable among members of the same biological family, appropriate also in the Christian worship setting where their family relationship under God was particularly expressed.

Participation

The intimacy of fellowship was in principle to be extended to all members of the church, regardless of their individual social status, economic standing and gender. 'There is no longer Jew or Greek, there is no longer slave or free, there is no longer male or female; for all of you are one in Christ Jesus', says the Apostle Paul (Gal. 3:38; cf. Col. 3:11). Although in its immediate context this statement functions as part of Paul's discussion of the full enfranchisement of Gentile converts along with Jewish Christians as members of God's redeemed people, children of Abraham, all of whom belong to Christ, it is clear that Paul here also represents the ideals to be reflected in the worship gatherings of the early Christian movement.

Thus, for example, although elsewhere Paul urges the retention of a gender distinction in the hairstyles of men and women, he also specifically mentions both genders participating in corporate worship through such actions as public prayer and prophecy (1 Cor. 11:2–16, esp. v. 6). Moreover, in Paul's discussion of the diversity of spiritual gifts that can be manifested publicly in worship (1 Cor. 12:1–31) there is no

---

[11] Banks, *Paul's Idea of Community: The Early House Churches in their Historical Setting*, esp. 33–42, 52–70.

indication that social status or gender makes any difference.[12] Instead, the impression we get is that divinely enabled contributions might come from anyone whom God chooses, and likely from a variety of people. The prophetic promise from Joel is cited as explanatory of the phenomena of earliest Christian religious experience, with God's Spirit manifested through sons and daughters, young and old, slaves and free (e.g., Acts 2:17, citing Joel 2:28–32). Indeed, in Acts 21:9 we are told specifically of the Christian leader Philip's four daughters who were believers and were endued with the prophetic gift. In Philippians 4:2–3, two women, Euodia and Syntyche, are named as leaders, and in Romans 16 about one-third of the numerous Christian leaders mentioned are women. It appears, thus, that earliest Christianity afforded significant opportunities for women to have visibility and respect as acknowledged leaders, including open participation in public liturgical life.

A similarly open attitude to participation by those of lower social and economic status, even slaves, including visible participation in corporate worship, seems to have been widespread among early Christian groups. As we would expect, the actual practice varied, and the social and economic stratification of the Roman world could manifest itself in the Christian worship setting. Thus Paul condemns the divisions and discrimination between the better off and the poor that had crept into the Corinthian celebration of the Lord's Supper (1 Cor. 11:17–22). But certainly the broad direction of Christian exhortation in the New Testament is toward a rather full participation in the worship gathering by people of either gender and of all social stations. From the success of the early Christian movement in recruiting converts of both genders and of various social and economic strata, it is reasonable to think that some significant level of fairly wide enfranchisement was manifested.

---

[12] The well-known verses in 14:34–35 now seem more likely to be an interpolation of a scribal marginal note and not the words of Paul. See, e.g., Fee, *The First Epistle to the Corinthians*, 696–708; Payne, 'Fuldensis, Sigla for Variants in Vaticanus, and 1 Cor. 14:34–35', *New Testament Studies* 41 (1995), 240–62.

Christian groups were not the only ones in which males and females and people of different social strata and nationalities could join in common cultic activities, but one of the prominent features of Christian worship was this breadth of participation.[13] Perhaps especially for women and those whose social status or ethnic background could prove a disadvantage, it was particularly meaningful to experience a corporate solidarity in worship that relativised or transcended the lines of differentiation and marginalisation operative in their life outside of the worship setting. Often, the leaders of the house churches may well have been those members of the little groups with comparatively more social skills, suitable experience and more education, who were more accustomed to exercising such roles. That is, they were likely often those of somewhat better social and economic backgrounds. But there was, of course, no hereditary priesthood, indeed in the first century no Christian priestly order at all. Worship in earliest Christian groups was comparatively informal and in principle open to contributions from members as they believed themselves inspired and were perceived by others to be gifted by God.

Fervour

The sense of divine gifting, charisms of the Spirit of various sorts, together with the other religious ideas and claims put forth in early Christian proclamation and instruction gave fervency to earliest Christian worship. From reports of some other Roman-era religious groups, it is clear that exuberance, joy, a sense of encounter with the divine, and even strong religious ecstasy were often sought by devotees and were cultivated by various means in worship events. Christian groups

---

[13] On women's opportunities in Roman-era religion, see Kraemer, *Maenads, Martyrs, Matrons, Monastics: A Sourcebook on Women's Religions in the Greco-Roman World; id., Her Share of the Blessings: Women's Religions among Pagans, Jews, and Christians.*

did not have at their disposal the sorts of resources put to use by some other groups (and in later centuries appropriated also by Christianity) to provide devotees with powerful religious experiences or at least a sense of awe (e.g., elaborate ceremonies or impressive temples), but it is clear that a religious fervour often characterised earliest Christian worship and would have been an impressive, attractive and meaningful feature. Indeed, strong religious fervour in worship might well have helped to compensate for the other religious activities to be foregone and might have helped to maintain the commitment to Christian exclusivity in worship.

From Paul's discussion of the problems in the Corinthian worship practices, we gain a vivid sense of the fervency that could sometimes manifest itself in ways he deemed unhelpful. The variety of worship-centred activities mentioned in 1 Corinthians 14:26 all indicate worshippers who experience direct divine inspiration and exaltation. Not only 'revelation' and 'a tongue or an interpretation', but also the 'hymn' and 'lesson' are probably to be taken as somewhat spontaneous contributions believed to be inspired by the Spirit. There is a still larger list of phenomena in 1 Corinthians 12:4–11, including divinely inspired utterances of wisdom, knowledge, prophecy and tongues-speaking, gifts of healing and the working of miracles, and 'discernment of spirits' (which may associated with exorcism). Also, when Paul challenges the Galatian Christians about what they imagine the basis to be for the manifestations of the Spirit and the miracles wrought among them in Galatians 3:5, it is likely that he has in mind the worship gathering as the setting for such divine blessings. In Colossians 3:16 and Ephesians 5:18–20, the inspired teaching and admonishing and the grateful singing of 'psalms, hymns, and spiritual songs' to God are all probably to be understood as phenomena of gathered worship that illustrate the religious exaltation and fervency sought in the earliest Christian groups. In 1 Thessalonians 5:19–21, Paul urges the Thessalonian Christians not to 'quench the Spirit' and to make room for prophecy (albeit with appropriate discrimination between good and bad spiritual manifestations), and again it is probably the worship gathering that he has in mind as the occasion for such manifestations of religious fervour.[14]

The frequency of the term 'joy' (*chara*) and references to 'rejoicing' (*agalliaomai*) in the New Testament reflect the jubilation encouraged and experienced particularly (though not exclusively) in worship.[15] This joy was connected with the sense of direct encounter with God, a powerful sense of the 'numinous', the Spirit being seen as the vehicle through which God communicated himself directly and the worship setting as the characteristic occasion (e.g., Acts 2:46–47).[16]

Earliest Christian proclamation portrayed a dramatic redemption from divine judgement, a full enfranchisement of Gentile converts into the elect of the God of Israel, and an eschatological salvation to be consummated in Christ's return but already manifested in the gifts of the Spirit and the success of the proclamation itself. In a passage warning against apostasy, the author of Hebrews refers to Christians as 'those who have . . . been enlightened, and have tasted the heavenly gift, and have shared in the Holy Spirit, and have tasted the goodness of the word of God and the powers of the age to come' (Heb. 6:4–5). This phrasing demonstrates the very experiential nature of earliest Christian religiosity, and the sense of that religious experience as being fraught with great significance. The early Christians believed that they had 'tasted' heavenly things, had been given the Holy Spirit, and had experienced eschatological powers. These convictions, reinforced through powerful religious experiences, understandably issued in religious joy and fervour.[17]

---

[14] See Fee, *God's Empowering Presence: The Holy Spirit in the Letters of Paul*, esp. 883–95, 'The Spirit and Worship'.

[15] Beyreuther and Finkenrath, 'Joy, Rejoice' in Brown (ed.), *The New International Dictionary of New Testament Theology*, 352–61.

[16] Dunn, *Jesus and the Spirit*, 185–88, esp. 188.

[17] L. T. Johnson, *Religious Experience in Earliest Christianity* is a plea to New Testament scholars to take the religious experiences reflected in the New Testament more seriously in attempts to characterise early Christianity.

Joy and fervour does not sustain itself automatically but has to be stimulated and cultivated repeatedly. Moreover, life experiences are such that anomie, disorientation, and discouragement are predictable. The worship gathering was not only the scene in which Christian jubilation and fervour were collectively expressed, it was also a major occasion and means for renewing fervour through shared worship, praise and attendant phenomena. It requires little imagination or argumentation to see that religious enthusiasm is more effectively cultivated and maintained through collective acts of affirmation and celebration. The exhortation in Hebrews 10:19–25 to persevere makes it crucial for believers not to neglect their assembling for worship and, thereby, mutual encouragement.

Significance

Although the house-church setting of earliest Christian worship was domestic and simple, believers were encouraged to attach a profound significance to their gatherings. In large part, this significance is connected to their collective significance as the redeemed. Paul teaches the Corinthian converts to think of themselves collectively as God's plantation (1 Cor. 3:5–9); God's building, with Jesus as their foundation (3:10–15); and as God's temple indwelt by the divine Spirit; and he warns them that divisive threats to the unity of the congregation are thus sacrilege (3:16–17).[18] In this notion of the gathered church as God's temple, the New Testament shows an analogy to similar views of the Qumran community.[19] In other texts we are told that Christian believers have been chosen by God and destined from before creation for an eschatological inheritance (Eph. 1:3–14). Indeed, they have already been exalted and given heavenly status with Christ

---

[18] Gärtner, *The Temple and Community in Qumran and the New Testament*; McKelvey, *The New Temple: The Church in the New Testament*.

[19] In addition to Gärtner's, *Temple and Community*, study, see also Klinzing, *Die Umdeutung des Kultus in der Qumrangemeinde und im Neuen Testament*.

(Eph. 2:4–7) and made 'citizens with the saints and also members of the household of God', thus forming a 'holy temple in the Lord' where God himself shall dwell (Eph. 2:19–22). As God's temple, made up of 'living stones', and as a 'holy priesthood', they offer 'spiritual sacrifices acceptable to God through Jesus Christ' in their collective worship (1 Pet. 2:4–5). Christ has made Christians 'a kingdom, priests to his God and Father' (Rev. 1:6), and they are promised such things as 'the crown of life' (Rev. 2:10), 'authority over the nations' (2:26), and a place with Christ on his throne (3:21). The author of Hebrews speaks of participation in the community of Christian believers in awesome terms:

> You have come to Mount Zion and to the city of the living God, the heavenly Jerusalem, and to innumerable angels in festal gathering, and to the assembly of the firstborn who are enrolled in heaven, and to God the judge of all, and to the spirits of the righteous made perfect, and to Jesus, the mediator of a new covenant, and to the sprinkled blood that speaks a better word than the blood of Abel. (Heb. 12:23–24).

Given that Christians were taught to think of themselves collectively in such terms, it is understandable that their cultic gatherings were seen as filled with meaning and significance as well. They did not have temple structures or the elaborate rituals familiar in the larger religious environment, but (perhaps, indeed, therefore) the gathered group was itself a living shrine and their praise and worship spiritual sacrifices pleasing to God. They did not have a priestly order; instead, they saw themselves collectively as a priesthood, all of them thus specially sacred and their gathering a holy occasion.

They experienced their assemblies as not merely human events but as having a transcendent dimension. They sensed God as directly and really present in their meetings through his Spirit. Indeed, even a gathering of two or three believers is graced with the presence of Christ (Matt. 18:20), giving it efficacy in prayer and other actions. In 1 Corinthians 11:10, the curious passing reference to the angels as present in the worship assembly shows how familiar the idea was. Paul's Corinthian readers apparently needed no further explanation (though we could wish for one!).[20] As the 'holy ones' (saints) of God, believers saw their worship gatherings as attended by heavenly 'holy ones', angels, whose presence signified the heavenly significance of their humble house-church assemblies. It is this sense that Christian collective worship participates in the heavenly cultus that finds later expression in the traditional words of the liturgy: 'Wherefore, with angels and archangels, and with all the company of heaven, we do laud and magnify your glorious name.' Scholars have suggested similarities with the Qumran sect, who seem to have thought of their worship as likewise a participation in heavenly angelic cultus, and thus as blessed with the presence of angels.[21] The point is that in their sense of their worship gatherings as an extension of and participation in the idealised worship of the heavenly hosts, and in their view of their gatherings as graced with God's holy angels, they express a vivid transcendent significance pertaining to these occasions.

Collective worship was also experienced as having a strong eschatological significance. In fact, for religious groups with a strong sense of heavenly realities and eschatological hopes, worship is logically seen as the occasion when heavenly realities come to expression on earth and when foretastes of eschatological hopes are experienced in the present. In ancient Jewish and Christian eschatology, what is hoped for is a triumph on earth of God's rule that is always secure in heaven: 'Your kingdom come, your will be done on earth as it is in heaven.' The prophet John pictures the eschatological consummation as the heavenly Jerusalem coming down to earth,

[20] The best treatments of the verse I know of are Hooker, 'Authority on Her Head: An Examination of 1 Cor 11:10', *New Testament Studies* 10, and Fitzmyer, 'A Feature of Qumran Angelology and the Angels of 1 Cor 11:10' in Fitzmyer, *The Semitic Background of the New Testament*.

[21] Noll, 'Angelology in the Qumran Texts', esp. 184–99; Davidson, *Angels at Qumran: A Comparative Study of 1 Enoch 1–36, 72–108 and Sectarian Writings from Qumran*; Mach, *Entwicklungsstadien des jüdischen Engelglaubens in vorrabbinischer Zeit*, 216–40; Jaubert, *La notion d'alliance dans le judaïsme aux abords d l'ère chrétienne*, 189–97.

wherein God will dwell (Rev. 21:1–4). Consequently, just as worship can be the occasion in which heaven and earth are specially joined, the earthly worship setting thus acquiring a transcendent dimension, so worship can be seen by devotees as a present, albeit provisional, realisation of conditions hoped for permanently in the age to come.

Once again, the Qumran sect provides us with a contemporary analogy as a first-century Jewish religious group with strong eschatological hopes who saw their worship in such terms.[22] In a very interesting study of the New Testament, Qumran texts, and the collection of early Christian songs called *The Odes of Solomon*, David Aune showed that religious groups can hold zealously to futurist eschatological hopes and can also have a strong sense of what scholars term 'realised eschatology', and that the latter outlook is characteristically linked with the cultic setting.[23]

Believing themselves to be the elect who have been granted salvation from the coming divine wrath and are promised participation in eschatological salvation (e.g., 1 Thess. 1:9–10; Rom. 8:18–23), earliest Christians experienced the divine Spirit as the 'first fruits' (Rom. 8:23) and initial instalment or deposit (2 Cor. 1:22) of eschatological salvation. In their worship occasions, when the Spirit was particularly and demonstrably experienced by them, they felt vividly the powers of the coming age, and saw their worship rituals as anticipations of eschatological hopes.

It is, for example, commonly accepted by scholars that among the meanings attached to earliest Eucharist meals was an eschatological significance, the church meal prefiguring the messianic banquet at which Jesus would preside.[24] To be sure,

---

[22] H.-W. Kuhn, *Enderwartung und gegenwärtiges Heil: Untersuchungen zu den Gemeindeliedern von Qumran*.

[23] Aune, *The Cultic Setting of Realized Eschatology in Early Christianity*.

[24] See, e.g., Cullmann, 'The Meaning of the Lord's Supper in Primitive Christianity', 5–23; McCormick, *The Lord's Supper: A Biblical Interpretation*, 88–107; Marshall, *Last Supper and Lord's Supper*, 146–55.

the Eucharist is also associated with Jesus' redemptive death, but both his passion and the Eucharist are set within an eschatological expectation and thereby are themselves given eschatological significance, as reflected in Paul's statement that in the meal believers 'proclaim the Lord's death *until he comes*' (1 Cor. 11:26).

Likewise, we should understand that the Christian ritual practice of confession/acclamation of Jesus as Lord, which was apparently a characteristic feature of earliest corporate worship both in Greek-speaking (e.g., Rom 10:9–10; 1 Cor. 12:3) and Aramaic-speaking groups (as indicated by the *maranatha* formula in 1 Cor. 16:22), was intended by them as anticipating the universal acclamation and reverence of Jesus as Lord that was central in their eschatological hopes (e.g., Phil. 2:9–11).[25] In their view, Jesus has already been exalted to God's right hand and commissioned to receive the submission of all things (1 Cor. 15:20–28). In their corporate acclamation and confession of Jesus' lordship, they were ritually constituting their worship-circle as offering that submission and thus as an anticipatory expression and locally defined realisation of God's ultimate purposes.

Their initiation ritual, baptism, was invested with enormous significance as well.[26] It was not simply an act of individual obedience, but was to be seen as signifying a powerful connection of believers with Jesus' death and resurrection that was to issue in an eschatological 'newness of life' expressed in the present in moral transformation (Rom. 6:1–4), and ultimately in the full resurrection life of the age to come. Through baptism, converts were joined in one spiritual body, thus transcending their individual differences of nationality or social status (1 Cor. 12:12–13). Once again, a ritual of a fairly simple nature was assigned a considerable depth of meaning. Indeed, as with a

---

[25] R. P. Martin, *An Early Christian Confession: Philippians 2.5–11 in Recent Interpretation*. See Michel, '[ʔo]μολογεω', in Kittel and Friedrich (eds.), *Theological Dictionary of the New Testament*, esp. 215–17, for the place of faith-confession as liturgical act.

[26] On baptism, see, e.g., Meeks, *First Urban Christians*, 150–57, and the discussion of the practice in my next chapter.

number of features of Christian worship, it may have been necessary to thematise heavily their rather simple rituals and invest them with quite exalted significance precisely because in themselves the rituals did not have the outwardly impressive features of the cultic practices of the pagan religious environment.

The terms used to refer to the Christian gathering and its activities also suggest an effort to invest them with large significance. The term used to refer especially to the gathering of Christian believers, *ekklesia*, is an interesting choice for a self-designation by early Christian groups. There were a number of frequently used terms available such as *thiasos* (the characteristic term for a group of persons who associated for the worship of a particular deity[27]), *eranos* (a fellowship to hold religious feasts to which participants contributed), *koinon* (a fellowship), or *synodos* (a group following a particular teaching), but so far as we can tell the term *ekklesia* is not among them.[28]

In its historic Greek usage, *ekklesia* designated the gathering of citizens of a city to conduct civic business. Such events always had a religious character and would be commenced with offerings to the gods, but the *ekklesia* was not a gathering precisely to conduct worship. An Ephesian inscription from 103–4 CE calls for images of gods to be set up on pedestals in the theatre for every *ekklesia*, which illustrates how such official gatherings of the competent citizens of a city to conduct important business was also nominally done under the authority of, and with respect for, the gods.[29] As Adolf Deissmann noted, *ekklesia* was actually taken over into Latin as a loan word prior to Christian influence, though there were certainly Latin terms for 'assembly', which indicates that the term *ekklesia* had a special connotation of importance recognised by Latin speakers that could not easily be communicated by translating the word.[30]

---

[27] Hammond and Scullard, *The Oxford Classical Dictionary*, s.v. 'Thiasos'.

[28] Coenen, *New International Dictionary of New Testament Theology*, 291–92.

[29] Deissmann, *Light from the Ancient East*, 112–3.

[30] Ibid., 112–13.

The other important use of *ekklesia* outside the New Testament is in the Greek Old Testament (the Bible of most early Christians, whether Jews or Gentiles) where it is regularly used to refer to Israel as the 'congregation' of the Lord (*ekklesia Kyriou*, e.g., Deut. 23:2 1 Chron. 28:8, most often translating the Hebrew term *qahal*). In the Old Testament usage, *ekklesia* designates Israel summoned by God to assemble for some act of obedience. But, though the term had this biblical usage, it was not used by Jews in the Roman period for their religious gatherings, for which the term *synagoge* (also used in the LXX) was the preferred Greek term.[31]

So, it appears that early Christians deliberately adopted and preferred a distinctive self-designation, a term not used by pagan or Jewish religious groups to refer to their cultic gatherings, yet a term whose pre-Christian usage connoted official significance and, in the Old Testament, a special religious association. More specifically, the term reflects the self-understanding of early Christian groups as being a legitimate continuation and heirs of Old Testament Israel, and also as assemblies of God's people, summoned by God to obedience and service, proclaiming God's kingdom in this world. In the use of the term *ekklesia* for the worship gatherings (used both for the 'whole church' of Christians in a given city, e.g., Acts 5:11; Rom. 16:23; 1 Cor 14:23, and for the house-church groups, e.g., Rom 16:5; 1 Cor. 16:19; Col. 4:15), we have an indication of the effort to invest these otherwise modest gatherings with a high meaning, which, among other things, would have helped members to find in them a rationale for making Christian worship their sole religious association.

Another term that probably carried an official-sounding significance is the adjective *kyriakos*, used in the New Testament by Paul to refer to the sacred meal as the 'Lord's Supper' (1 Cor. 11:20), and in Revelation to refer to Sunday as 'the Lord's Day' (Rev. 1:10). *Kyriakos* is used in other early Christian writings as well, showing its wide appropriation (*Magnes.*

---

[31] For discussion and citation of sources, see Schmidt, *Theological Dictionary of the New Testament*, 'ἐκκλησια', esp. 513–18; Coenen, *Dictionary of New Testament Theology*, 291–307.

9:1; *Did.* 14:1; *Gos.Pet.* 9:35; 12:50). I consider Deissmann's proposals made several decades ago to be correct, that the term derives from Roman imperial usage to designate things as belonging/pertaining to the emperor (e.g., 'the imperial treasury' [*ton kyriakon logon*], 'imperial service' [*tas kyriakas hyperesias*]).[32] First-century Christians, whether Jews or Gentiles, would have known this imperial usage and connotation, and so the adoption of the term would very likely have communicated to them the high significance claimed for the sacred meal and that the day of assembly was official and important. Indeed, Deissmann offered the intriguing suggestion that the appropriation of this term from 'the official vocabulary of Imperial law' to designate the day for Christian assembly and the religious meal of that assembly 'may have been connected with conscious feelings of protest against the cult of the Emperor with its 'Augustus Day' [*Sebaste*]'.[33] It certainly seems to me difficult to avoid the impression that the term *kyriakos* functioned to attribute to Christian worship practices an importance of the highest order.

Potency

When discussing the religious fervour of earliest Christian worship, I mentioned such phenomena as prophecy and miracles of healing. The point I wish to make here is that such phenomena also exhibit the potency believed by earliest Christians to be available and operative in their gathered worship. That is, for earliest Christians the worship event was not merely a religious exercise by the participants, an opportunity to re-affirm their beliefs and to engage in ritualised behaviour; it was an occasion for the manifestation and experience of

---

[32] Deissmann, Bible Studies, 217–19; id., Ancient East, 357–61. See also, e.g., Bauer, et al., A Greek-English Lexicon of the New Testament and Other Early Christian Literature, 458, s.v. 'κυριακος'; MM 364, s.v. 'κυριακος' for examples.

[33] Deissmann, *Ancient East*, 359.

divine powers.[34] Indeed, it appears that expectations were characteristically high that in the worship setting God would be encountered in demonstrative fashion. In the context of a lengthy discussion of proper attitudes and practices in worship in 1 Corinthians 12–14, Paul refers to various 'gifts' (*charismata*) of the Spirit, various forms of 'service' (*diakoniai*) and various 'operations' *(energemata*, a Greek term consistently used in the New Testament to refer to phenomena attributed to supernatural forces) of God (1 Cor. 12:4–6).[35]

The communication that went on in early Christian worship included the experience of God speaking in the utterances of Christian prophets, and related phenomena.[36] In 1 Corinthians 12:4–11, Paul uses several expressions to refer to utterances experienced as directly inspired by God's Spirit, including 'a word of wisdom' and 'a word of knowledge' (v. 8), 'prophecy', 'kinds of tongues' and 'interpretation of tongues' (v. 10). Similarly, in 1 Corinthians 14:6, where Paul advises against uninterpreted tongues-speaking in corporate worship because it cannot be understood and thus cannot edify, he prefers that one speak 'in some revelation or knowledge or prophecy or teaching'. It is difficult for us to distinguish with confidence the phenomena to which these various terms refer, and it may in fact be that Paul does not intend them to be taken as mutually exclusive types of utterance. Whatever the relation may be between 'prophecy', 'a word of knowledge', 'a word of wisdom', 'a revelation', and the other terms that seem to refer to inspired utterances, it is clear that verbal manifestations of divine power were experienced frequently. In fact, at least in the Corinthian church gathering, verbal manifestations of the Spirit were so much a feature that Paul felt it necessary to give regulations for their orderly operation.

---

[34] See L. T. Johnson's emphasis on the sense of divine power reflected in New Testament texts (*Religious Experience*, e.g., 6–12).
[35] Dunn, *Jesus and the Spirit*, 199–258.
[36] Aune, *Prophecy in Early Christianity and the Ancient Mediterranean World*; Gillespie, *The First Theologians: A Study in Early Christian Prophecy*.

From the directions he gives to the Corinthians about the exercise of prophecy in the church gathering in 1 Corinthians 14:29–33, we can gather that there were often multiple prophets in a given group, and that the prophecy came by 'revelation'. In Acts 13:1–3 we are given a picture of how prophetic utterances could come in the worship setting and were taken as the words of God's Spirit coming through the inspired individuals, in this case giving directions to commission Paul and Barnabas for itinerant mission work.[37]

In addition to divine power expressed in prophetic speech, there is also reference to 'miracles' operative in earliest Christian groups. The usual Greek term so translated is *dynameis*, the plural form of the Greek word for 'power', and so the original connotation was phenomena seen as special and very direct manifestations of God's power, 'powerful/mighty events/works'. In 1 Corinthians 12:10 Paul lists 'workings of miracles' (*energemata dynameon*) as one of the various types of things that God does in the church gathering, and in Galatians 3:5 he points the Galatian Christians to God's distribution of the Spirit and working of miracles among them as proof of the validity of their religious standing. Both epistles are addressed to groups of believers and were intended to be read in their worship gatherings. It seems most cogent, therefore, to take the worship gathering to be the characteristic setting in which 'miracles' were expected.

Quite what Paul was referring to is not clear to us, however. Again, as with the utterances phenomena, it may be that we should not think of 'miracles' as a restricted and very specific label. The term may more likely be intended as a general term

---

[37] We need not detain ourselves with the question of the historicity of this particular episode. Even if one suspects a fictional narrative (or the author's hand in supplying details) here, in order to make such an episode credible the author of Acts clearly had to reflect the sort of phenomena with which his original readers would have been familiar, thus giving us at least a general and indirect indication of the sorts of things that likely went on in first-century Christian worship gatherings.

for a certain spectrum of phenomena that were experienced as direct and impressive manifestations of divine power.

Among these may well have been the 'gifts of healings' that Paul mentions in 1 Corinthians 12:9. Readers of the New Testament will be acquainted with the stories of miraculous healings in the gospels' accounts of Jesus' ministry and the activities of Christian leaders in Acts. In these cases healings are placed in the context of proclamation and mission (e.g., Acts 3:1–10; 5:12–16; 9:32–35; 14:8–18). But, as James 5:14–18 indicates, miraculous healing was also seen as something available to be sought by and for believers in the context of the Christian fellowship.[38] Moreover, Paul's mention of healings in 1 Corinthians 12:9 is in the context of other phenomena of the Christian worship gathering, and in a larger context devoted to issues of propriety in and proper attitudes toward the worship gathering (1 Cor. 11–14). Furthermore, Paul explicitly states in 12:7 that each of the types of divine manifestations he mentions is given 'for the common good', which most likely means that these phenomena are here set within the context of the gathered church. Consequently, I think we must conclude that miraculous healings were among the manifestations of divine power experienced in the *ekklesia*.[39]

Other references suggest that the gathered *ekklesia* could experience divine power in more ominous ways. To stay with Pauline material, there is the curious passage in 1 Corinthians 5:1–8 concerning a man in the Corinthian church living sexually with 'his father's wife'. We cannot linger over the several intriguing difficulties in this passage.[40] For our purposes, the

---

[38] Those addressed in James 5:14–18 are clearly believers, who are encouraged to call for the 'elders' of their Christian group to anoint them and pray for their healing. The reference to the powerful efficacy of prayer (v. 16) and the citation of the example of Elijah's prayer for rain (v. 17–18) seem clearly to reflect a view of the healing proffered as miraculous.

[39] On 1 Cor. 12:4–11, see the excellent discussion in Fee, *Corinthians*, 582–600.

[40] Again, see the full discussion in Fee, *Corinthians*, 198–214.

relevant matter is the way that Paul refers to the nature of the Christian assembly and the action that he commands. Having made a judgement about this case, Paul orders the church to gather in the name of the Lord Jesus (v. 4) and 'hand this man over to Satan for the destruction of the [or his] flesh in order that the [or his] spirit may be saved in the day of the Lord' (v. 5). Gathered in Jesus' name, they meet 'with the power of our Lord Jesus' present also (v. 4), and thus empowered are able to carry out the judgement, which involves not merely a severing of the offender from the fellowship of the *ekklesia* (vv. 9–13) but also an exercise of spiritual power that may be phenomenologically likened in some ways to a ritual curse. By the power of Jesus, a power invoked through the ritual use of Jesus' name, the offender is given up to Satanic affliction, though, it appears, with a longer-term redemptive aim that may have included the offender's repentance.[41]

Here we surely have a dramatic example of the potency that first-century Christians could see associated with the gathered *ekklesia*. In their experience, it is divine power, the power of the Lord Jesus, operative in his name, and particularly manifest in their *gathering*. The same power that could be experienced in 'miracles' of a beneficial nature, in revelation, prophecy and other inspired utterances is here invoked to carry out judgement against an offender.

In 1 Corinthians 11:27–32, Paul warns Christian believers about the danger of eating and drinking judgement against themselves through the abuses of the Lord's Supper that he condemns, and refers to 'many who are weak and ill and some have died' as manifestations of divine judgement arising from such abuses. The logic seems to be that, as the Lord's Supper,

---

[41] Schillington, 'Atonement Texture in 1 Corinthians 5.5', *Journal for the Study of the New Testament* 71 (1998), 29–50, reviews recent discussion of this verse and argues that the verse does not anticipate the restoration of the offender but the purification and preservation of the church. Of course Paul was concerned about the latter, but I am not persuaded by Schillington's own interpretation of the verse. See my discussion of this passage in the next chapter of this book.

the Christian sacred meal is an event where Christ is present in power for good toward those believers who are aligned with his purposes and for potential judgement toward those who do not recognise that the gathered *ekklesia* is (and is to be treated as) the Lord's 'body'.

Summary

We began this discussion by noting that for pagan converts Christian worship was to be the only approved form of cultic devotion from among the rich variety on offer in the Roman-era environment. Given this, it is all the more important to consider what may have characterised earliest Christian worship, what was 'on offer' there so to speak, and how Christian worship was meaningful to adherents. It is clear that, in spite of the rather severe and unusual demand for an exclusive devotional commitment, the early Christian movement succeeded in winning converts. We cannot say that the worship of Christian groups was in itself a factor in Christian evangelism, but to hold their converts, Christian fellowship and the corporate religious life within that fellowship had to be sufficiently meaningful and satisfying to suffice for the range of religious activities they were expected to forego.

To emphasise, as I have in this chapter, the qualities and features of early Christian worship is by no means to imply that these features were all unique to Christian groups. 'Pagan' worship of the time also offered powerful inducements and satisfying features for participants. In its various forms and settings, these features could include such things as a sense of belonging and intimacy, and rituals endowed with great significance. My aim in this chapter has been to show that, though early Christian worship was fairly simple and unimpressive in comparison with the more elaborate religious practices of the Roman period, it too offered features that likely addressed the religious, personal and social needs of believers.

I contend that the features we have considered here help us to see what earliest Christians got out of their worship and what features may have offset for them the plainness and comparative simplicity of their cultic setting and rituals. The small size and domestic setting offered an intimacy of association in worship. The openness to many types of contributions to worship and to inspired gifts manifested by men and women and by people of various social levels offered participants a sense of direct involvement and participation. The strong sense of the Christian worship assembly as the prime occasion for the Spirit's manifestation in demonstrative forms and the heightened sense of the significance of their groups both reflected and promoted a strong religious fervour. These little house-groups saw themselves as bearing salvation-historical significance, their meetings constituting God's *ekklesia* called together in response to the divine summons issued in the gospel message. Their worship assembly was itself an event of eschatological meaning, a foretaste of the blessings of the coming age, and partook of heavenly realities, including the presence of holy angels and the presence and power of Christ experienced through the phenomena that they saw as manifestations of divine power.

Chapter 3

The Binitarian Shape of Early Christian Worship

Having looked at some general features of earliest Christian worship in the preceding chapter, I now wish to focus on what we may call its 'binitarian shape'. By this term I refer to the inclusion of Christ with God (the 'Father') as recipient of the worship.[1] To be sure, the further fruition of Christian worship traditions led to all three persons of the Trinity (the 'Father', 'Son', and 'Holy Spirit') coming to be worshipped as one God. But in the earliest observable stages of Christian worship in the New Testament, devotion is offered to God the Father and to (and through) Jesus. The Holy Spirit is certainly often referred to as the agent of divine power in and among believers, and as the mode of divine enablement and presence specifically in worship. In the New Testament, worship is

---

[1] Of the many studies of worship in the New Testament, I cite the following as broadly useful: Bradshaw, *The Search for the Origins of Christian Worship*; Cabaniss, *Pattern in Early Christian Worship*; Cullmann, *Early Christian Worship*; Delling, *Worship in the New Testament*; Hahn, *The Worship of the Early Church*; R. P. Martin, *Worship in the Early Church*; id., 'Worship', in Hawthorne and Martin (eds.) *Dictionary of Paul and His Letters*; id., 'Worship and Liturgy', in Martin and Davids (eds.) *Dictionary of the Later New Testament and its Developments*; Moule, *Worship in the New Testament*; Nielen, *Gebet und Gottesdienst im Neuen Testament*. The more recent survey of issues by Aune is especially worth attention: 'Worship, Early Christian', in Freedman, D.N. (ed.), *Anchor Bible Dictionary*.

offered in the Holy Spirit, but it is not so clear that the Spirit is seen as the recipient of worship. In noting this, I am not adopting any critical stance as regards the later and more developed trinitarian worship practices of Christian tradition. My point is simply the historical observation that at its earliest observable stage Christian *worship* was more 'binitarian', with devotion directed to God and Christ. Earliest Christian religious experience involved God, Christ and the Spirit; but the devotional pattern was more 'binitarian' as to the divine recipients of worship.[2]

Before we go into the discussion further, I must address one more matter. Over the last ten years or so especially, there has been very vigorous investigation and debate about the origins and background of the worship of Christ.[3] A great deal of valuable work has been done, especially the investigation of the Jewish religious matrix out of which earliest Christianity developed.[4] But it seems to me that the discussion has been

---

[2] Indeed, it appears that Christian worship has remained functionally 'binitarian', with the great majority of hymns, prayers, and other components of worship and devotion directed to God and Christ. Granted, in the developed theology of the Christian tradition the Holy Spirit is also formally declared a recipient of worship, as reflected in the Nicene-Constantinopolitan Creed (381 CE): 'And [I believe] in the Holy Spirit . . . who with the Father and the Son together is worshipped and glorified.' For text and discussion, see, e.g., Schaff, *The Creeds of Christendom*, 1: 24–29; Leith, *Creeds of the Churches*, 31–33. But this takes us considerably beyond the very early years with which we are concerned here.

[3] Three works in particular can be cited as stimulating this discussion: Segal, *Two Powers in Heaven: Early Rabbinic Reports about Christianity and Gnosticism*; Bauckham, 'The Worship of Jesus in Apocalyptic Christianity', *New Testament Studies* 27 (1981), 322–41; Hurtado, *One God, One Lord: Early Christian Devotion and Ancient Jewish Monotheism*. In June 1998, St. Andrews University hosted the International Conference on the Historical Origins of the Worship of Jesus, reflecting the salience of the topic in recent scholarship.

[4] In the preface to the second edition of *One God, One Lord* I briefly discuss a number of studies that appeared in the ten years between the first and second editions.

plagued by insufficient clarity of definitions of key categories and terms. Before we proceed to this examination of early Christian worship practices, therefore, it may be helpful to state and briefly defend the definitions of some key terms that I will use.

Worship

The English word 'worship' and its translation equivalents in koine Greek have a wide range of semantic possibilities. So, when one claims that this or that figure is given 'worship', it is not always or automatically clear what is meant. In the traditional marriage service of the *Book of Common Prayer*, for example, when the groom places the wedding ring on his bride's finger he promises, 'with my body I thee worship', which essentially represents a commitment to sexual fidelity and loving respect for his wife. Coming as it does in a formal service of Christian matrimony, no deification of the bride is implied, and no violation of Christian monotheism need be feared! More generally, dictionary definitions of the noun run from 'courtesy or reverence paid to worth; hence honour; respect' to 'act of paying divine honours to a deity', and 'obsequious respect or devotion'.[5]

A similar semantic range attaches to several of the relevant Greek terms, especially if one takes into account their usage in various bodies of evidence and situations. In the biblical texts, however, the words tend to be used with greater frequency in connection with reverence directed toward a figure that is treated as a deity. In the NT, the verb *latreuo* (21 uses) and its noun cognate, *latreia* (5 uses), are connected exclusively with God (or other deities) as object.[6] Likewise, *threskeia* (4 uses) consistently in the NT denotes religious devotion offered to a

---

[5] *The Book of Common Prayer* (London: Mowbray), 'The Form of Solemnisation of Matrimony'. *Webster's New Collegiate Dictionary* (Springfield, Mass.: Merriam, 1961) s.v. 'worship'.
[6] Strathmann, 'λατρεύω, λατρεία', in Kittel and Friedrich (eds.), *Theological Dictionary of the New Testament*.

deity.[7] The verb *leitourgeo* and its noun cognate, *leitourgia*, appear only a few times in the NT and (likely showing the influence of the LXX usage) in all cases refer directly to cultic/worship activity (Luke 1:23; Acts 13:2; Heb. 8:6; 9:21; 10:11) or to other religious acts where the intention is clearly to imbue the acts with a cultic flavour (Rom. 15:27; 2 Cor. 9:12; Phil. 2:17, 30).[8] Indded, with several of these terms, the actions connoted seem to include more than specific cultic ones, and take in a range of religious devotion intended as expressions of service offered to deity.[9]

The most frequent verb, however, *proskyneo* (used 60 times in the New Testament), in its many Septuagint uses can describe reverence or respect given to a variety of figures where no deification of the recipient seems implied:[10] Ruth to Boaz (Ruth 2:10), Joseph's brothers to Joseph (Gen. 37:9, 10, et al.), a petitioner to a prophet/holy man (2 Kings 2:15; 4:37), a subject to a king (1 Sam. 24:9; 1 Kings 1:16, 23, 31; 1 Chron. 21:21), Moses to his father-in-law (Exod. 18:7), and others who show deep respect for a superior or one from whom they seek kindness (e.g., Jacob to Esau, Gen. 33:3–7; Abraham to the Hittites, Gen. 23:7, 12; a Cushite messenger to Joab, 2 Sam. 18:21; the dishonest servant begging mercy from his king, Matt. 18:26). Indeed, Moses prophesies that

---

[7] Schmidt, 'θρησκεία, etc', in Kittel and Friedrich (eds.), *Theological Dictionary*.

[8] Strathmann and Meyer, 'Λειτουργέω, λειτουργία', in Kittel and Friedrich (eds.), *Theological Dictionary*.

[9] Scholars debate whether Col. 2:18 (*threskeia ton angellon*) refers to the worship offered *by* angels or the accusation of worship offered *to* angels, but either way the term connotes cultic reverence offered as to deities. John 16:2 warns that Jews will even deem the killing of Jesus' followers as 'offering worship to God' (*latreian prospherein to theo*).

[10] Greeven, 'προσκυνέω,προσκυνητής'. in Kittel and Friedrich (eds.), *Theological Dictionary*. The most complete study of the phenomenon of *proskynesis* is still Horst, *Proskynein: Zur Anbetung im Urchristentum nach ihrer religionsgeschichtlichen Eigenart*, which has not been sufficiently noted by some in current discussions of early Christian worship.

the Egyptians will reverence him as they beseech him to take the Israelites with him and depart Egypt (Exod. 11:8).

In the most emphatically monotheistic passages of the Bible, the elect are promised that they will be shown reverence by Gentiles in recognition of God's uniqueness and his favour upon Israel (Isa. 45:14–15; 49:7, 23). It is this promise of the vindication of the elect that is likely alluded to in Revelation 3:9, where the Philadelphian Christians are promised that their opponents will reverence them with the same gesture that the nations will use to give obeisance to God in Revelation 15:4. Incidentally, it seems to me most likely that the passages in the 'Similitudes' of *1 Enoch* where the 'Son of Man' figure is reverenced by the nations (48:5; 62:1–9) are to be taken as directly indebted to these same passages from Isaiah. Thus, for the author of *1 Enoch* the obeisance given to the 'Son of Man' no more connoted cultic worship or deification of this figure than did the equivalent descriptions of obeisance given to Israel/the servant/the elect in Isaiah or promised to the elect in Revelation.

But certainly in the Septuagint *proskyneo* also very frequently designates the act of reverence given to God or other deities (e.g., Exod. 20:5; 23:24; 34:8; 1 Sam. 1:3; Neh. 8:6; 9:3), and in the New Testament the term most often has this connotation. Of the remaining New Testament uses, in addition to two cases where Satan asks Jesus for reverence (Matt. 4:9; Luke 4:7), which probably represent the temptation to give Satan worship, one case where Peter is reverenced and objects to it (Acts 10:25), and one use in Hebrews 1:6, where angels are commanded to reverence the Son, there are another fifteen cases in the gospels where the term describes reverence given to Jesus either during his ministry (e.g., Mark 5:6; Matt. 20:20; cf. the mocking obeisance of Mark 15:19) or after his resurrection (Matt. 28:9, 17; Luke 24:52).

Given the range of reverence connoted by the gesture of *proskynesis* (the gesture indicated by the verb *proskyneo*) in its wider usage, it is not always easy to be sure as to what level of reverence for Jesus is indicated in particular cases where the 'pre-Easter' Jesus is given the gesture. Likewise, we should not take every instance of *proskynesis* of other figures in other sources as connoting the same thing as the cultic worship of a deity. In itself, the gesture (which originally involved bowing and a kiss-gesture) seems always to express reverence or respect for the figure to whom it is directed, but the specific meaning or significance of the reverence or respect varies with the nature and claims of the figure to whom the reverence is given. Thus, *proskynesis* to a royal official need mean only that one thereby demonstrates acceptance of the official as validly one's superior and as entitled to such respect. So, for example, Mordecai's refusal to reverence Haman (Esther 3:1–6) registers Mordecai's disdain for him and perhaps for the obsequious court style involved.[11]

We see something of the diversity or breadth of reverence that *proskynesis* can express vividly illustrated in 1 Chronicles 29:20–22, where the people bow and reverence both God and King David (v. 20b). Cultic worship here is given only to God, however, for David orders the people to 'Bless the \LORD your God' (v. 20a), and the sacrifices and offerings are given specifically to Yahweh (vv. 21–22). That *proskynesis* is also given to the king here seems to mean that he is reverenced as the rightful king who has God's approval, and so the king's commands to worship God are obeyed.[12] The reverence given to the king is not, however, the same as the worship given to God here, even though the same sort of gesture is used to express reverence for both.[13]

---

[11] It is likely that the author intends a contrast between the fawning reverence of Haman as chief royal official and the reference to Mordecai's elevation to a position next in rank to the king (Esth. 10:2), which Mordecai uses for the welfare of his people.

[12] On the treatment of the king by the Chronicler, see Kuntzmann, 'Le trône de Dieu dans l'oeuvre du chroniste' in Philonenko (ed.), *Le Trône de Dieu*.

[13] That Solomon is pictured as seated 'on the throne of the LORD' (1 Chron. 29:23) of course refers to him as sitting on the royal throne, which in a theocratic kingdom is a throne established by the deity, the king ruling by divine appointment and acting as a representative of the deity. Nothing in the passage indicates any confusion of the king with *Yahweh* or any offering of sacrifice or formal cultic worship to the king.

In the title of this chapter I use the term 'worship' to mean the actions of reverence intended to express specifically religious devotion of the sort given to a deity in the cultures or traditions most directly relevant to earliest Christianity. That is, I use the term to designate 'cultic' worship, especially devotion offered in a specifically worship (liturgical) setting and expressive of the thanksgiving, praise, communion and petition that directly represent, manifest and reinforce the relationship of the worshippers with the divine.[14] Inasmuch as the earliest Christians *met* as groups, I am particularly interested here in the religious devotion characteristic of these settings as a shared expression of their religious orientation and convictions. In addition, we shall consider features of devotional practice in other settings (e.g., personal prayer) to the extent that such features are openly referred to by early Christians and included by them as part of their shared devotional 'pattern'.[15] My concern is to analyse those devotional actions that represented for early Christians their most cherished religious convictions about the divine.

Binitarian

Given that the religious attitudes of earliest Christians were much shaped by biblical/Jewish scruples about avoiding the

---

[14] See, e.g., Muller, *Dictionary of Latin and Greek Theological Terms*, s.v. 'cultus', 'cultus vere divinus', 'latria'. Aune ('Worship, 975) cites S. Mowinckel's definition of 'cult' as 'the visible, socially arranged and ordered, efficacious forms through which the religious experience of communion between the deity and the 'community' is actualised and its effects expressed' (S. Mowinkel, *RGG* 4: 120–21).

[15] From evidence of later centuries, it is evident that at least some Christians engaged in religious or ritual actions beyond the 'liturgical' setting, including such things as spells, amulets, etc., and sometimes invoked figures other than, and in addition to, God and Christ. In the present discussion, however, I concentrate on the devotional actions openly encouraged, engaged in and affirmed by Christians as directly expressive of their religious identity. See, e.g., Aune, 'Magic in Early Christianity' in Temporini and Haase (eds.), *Aufstieg und Niedergang der römischen Welt;* also Meyer and Smith, *Ancient Christian Magic: Coptic Texts of Ritual Power.*

cultic worship of other gods, humans, angels, and any figures other than the one true God of the biblical tradition, the explicit and programmatic inclusion of Christ in their devotional practice is interesting, even striking, as I have demonstrated elsewhere.[16] In the next section of this discussion, we shall analyse the specific phenomena involved in the 'Christ-devotion' of early Christians. As I hope to show in the final section of this chapter, the inclusion of Christ as recipient of religious devotion was not intended by early Christians as recognising another god. Although 'di-theism' might well represent the sort of charge that at least some critics might have hurled at them (e.g., John 5:18; 10:33), the term does not seem to represent their own views of their devotional pattern. I propose that in this characteristic 'two-ishness' of their devotional practice there is also a pattern of religious behaviour that links Christ with God in ways that seem intended to maintain an exclusivist 'monotheistic' stance. It is this early Christian accommodation of Christ as an additional figure along with God ('the Father') within a strongly monotheistic religious commitment that I refer to as the 'binitarian' shape of Christian worship.[17]

The Phenomena of Early Cultic Christ-Devotion

I am uneasy with abstractions that cannot readily be tested, and am aware of the difficulties in understanding the unexpressed (or dimly expressed) conceptions of ancients and in avoiding anachronism in developing conceptual categories for the analysis of earliest Christian beliefs. Consequently, I have emphasised the importance of an inductive approach that

---

[16] See esp. Hurtado, *One God, One Lord*; *id.*, 'First-Century Jewish Monotheism', *Journal for the Study of the New Testament* 71 (1998), pp. 3–26.

[17] Some scholars use the term 'christological monotheism' to refer to the inclusion of Christ with God in early Christianity. See, e.g., Bauckham, *God Crucified: Monotheism and Christology in the New Testament*, esp. 25–42.

focuses on the actual phenomena of religious devotion.[18] Thus, in my book, *One God, One Lord* I dealt with early Christian devotional *practice* as directed toward Christ, and I referred to the evidence of a 'mutation' in monotheistic devotion in the earliest observable literary remains of first-century Christianity.[19] I listed and briefly discussed six phenomena of early Christian religious devotion, which I contended amounted to a pattern of devotion that was unparalleled among other known religious groups that identified themselves with the biblical/Jewish tradition. This pattern of devotion thus constitutes a distinctive 'mutation' in Jewish monotheistic practice, with a clearly 'binitarian' character.

In the eleven years since the first edition of that book, some scholars have questioned whether the phenomena really constituted a significant 'mutation' in monotheistic practice and really represented cultic worship of Christ. Some others, pointing to what they allege to be precedents and analogies, grant that early Christians worshipped Christ but question whether it was really as innovative and historically significant as I have claimed.[20] It is, therefore, appropriate for me to return to the specific phenomena of early 'Christ-devotion', which, I still contend, do collectively constitute a distinctive pattern of binitarian devotion in which Christ is included with God as a recipient of devotion that can properly be

---

[18] In 'First-Century Jewish Monotheism', for example, I urge an inductive approach to the definition of the term 'monotheism' as a descriptor of ancient Jewish and Christian religion.

[19] Hurtado, *One God, One Lord*, esp. 99–100, 124. For a useful discussion of worship practices/rituals in Pauline churches, see Meeks, *The First Urban Christians: The Social World of the Apostle Paul*, 140–63. On pagan religious/cultic practices, see MacMullen, *Paganism in the Roman Empire*, esp. 1–48. For a recent survey of earliest Jewish synagogue practice, see Reif, *Judaism and Hebrew Prayer: New Perspectives on Jewish Liturgical History*, esp. 53–87.

[20] Dunn (*The Theology of Paul the Apostle*, 257–60) prefers to describe Pauline Christ-devotion as 'veneration of Christ, meaning by that something short of full-scale worship'. Fletcher-Louis claims to have produced several precedents for the worship of Christ (*Luke–Acts: Angels, Christology and Soteriology*, 120–29, 214).

understood as worship.[21] As our concern here is primarily historical, I shall particularly draw attention to evidence of earliest observable stages of Christian devotional practice. This means concentrating on Pauline texts and such other references as may plausibly be taken as reflecting very primitive Christian practice.

In the light of criticisms of my positions, I wish to re-emphasise two things about the phenomena to be discussed. First, they are a *constellation* of devotional practices, and it is the collective force of the phenomena that constitutes the 'mutation' in monotheistic practice that I allege. For this or that individual phenomenon there may be interesting partial analogies. For example, it has been suggested that the invocation of angels in Jewish 'magical' material, or the reverential reference to them in other Jewish sources, may offer some sort of partial analogy for prayer to Jesus and ritual invocation of him.[22] But I am not aware that anyone has offered any analogy for the full *pattern* of devotional phenomena focused on Jesus.[23]

---

[21] See the valuable discussion by Bauckham, 'Jesus, Worship of,' for a very similar view of matters. Among earlier studies, cf. Conzelmann, 'Christus im Gottesdienst der neutestamentlichen Zeit', in Conzelmann, *Theologie als Schriftauslegung: Aufsätze zum Neuen Testament*, 120–30.

[22] See esp. Stuckenbruck, *Angel Veneration and Christology*, and my review in *JTS* 47 (1996): 248–53.

[23] Horbury (*Jewish Messianism and the Cult of Christ*) proposes that Jewish messianism provides the key that explains the worship of Christ. But, in fact, praise of Jewish rulers and honorific rhetoric concerning messianic figures provide no real parallel to the pattern of cultic devotion to Christ expressed in the New Testament. Horbury uses the term 'cult' so broadly as to make it cover almost any kind of respect and reverence given to a figure. This obfuscates matters. The same criticism can be levelled against Horbury's association of the worship of Christ and early Christian and Jewish reverence for martyrs ('The Cult of Christ and the Cult of the Saints', *New Testament Studies* 44 (1998), 444–69). Contra Horbury, *Mart.Poly.* 17:3 makes a clear distinction between the two types of reverence. Note also Irenaeus' statement: 'Nor does

Secondly, and perhaps even more importantly, these phenomena are the actual devotional practices of adherents of a known religious movement, and they functioned as the identifying marks of their devotional life. Scattered references to this or that figure receiving reverence in literary scenes placed in the cosmic past (e.g., the command to the angels to reverence Adam as God's 'image' in *Vitae Adae et Evae* 13–14), the eschatological future (e.g, the reverence given by foreign kings to the Elect One/Son of Man figure in *1 Enoch* 48:5; 62:9) or in a figurative vision set in a celestial plane (the obeisance of the stars to Moses in *Ezekiel the Tragedian*) are interesting as illustrating the speculative directions and forms that ancient Jewish thought could take toward exalted symbolic figures.[24] But none of the proffered examples offers us evidence of religious movements or groups whose devotional pattern actually included the offering of cultic reverence to any of these figures. Instead, these scenes showing reverence given to these various figures all appear to be only *literary* phenomena, and this means that the obeisance described is not properly 'worship' of the figures as deities by any actual group of devout Jews. In the case of the NT evidence about Christ-devotion, we have characteristics of the devotional *praxis* of the early Christian

---

[23] *(continued)* she [the church] perform anything by means of angelic invocations, or by incantations, or by any other wicked, curious art; but, directing her prayers to the Lord, who made all things, in a pure, sincere, and straightforward spirit, and calling upon the name of our Lord Jesus Christ, she is accustomed to work miracles for the advantage of mankind . . .' (*Against Heresies*, 2.32.5 [*ANF* 2.409]). The point is not whether all Christians consistently followed such a practice but what sort of devotional pattern was promoted as correct. Devotion to Christ was included, and devotion to other figures was not.

[24] Steenburg points to the scene in the Latin *VitAdEve*, but acknowledges that there is no evidence of any Jewish group practising a cultic reverence of Adam as their pattern of cultic devotion ('The Worship of Adam and Christ as the Image of God', *Journal for the Study of the New Testament* 39, [1990], 95–109). English translations of these and other extra-canonical writings are available in Charlesworth, *The Old Testament Pseudepigrapha*.

movement, with the reverence given as part of the cultic pattern of early Christian groups.

1. Prayer[25]

As is to be expected, in the New Testament and other early Christian sources prayer is most characteristically offered to God (e.g., Acts 4:24–30). But it is also equally characteristic that prayer is offered 'through' Jesus (e.g., Rom. 1:8) or in Jesus' name (e.g., John 16:23–24), something for which I know of no parallel in the evidence of ancient Jewish prayer practice. Indeed, in the NT prayer is often described as offered to 'the God and Father of our Lord Jesus Christ' (e.g., 2 Cor. 1:3; Eph. 1:3; Col. 1:3). The latter expression can be paralleled with references to 'the God of Abraham, the God of Isaac, and the God of Jacob' (Exod. 3:6; Mark 12:26), but this re-identification of God by reference to Jesus surely indicates the importance of Jesus in early Christian devotion as group identity-marker and as shaping the pattern of their piety.

Moreover, though it is not so frequent, we find evidence of prayer to Jesus, both jointly with God and directly to Jesus himself.[26] In Paul's letters, several passages which are technically prayer-wish expressions are probably to be taken as reflecting prayer practices in which God and Jesus were

---

[25] Major studies on early Christian prayer include Hamman, *La prière I. Le Nouveau Testament*; id., 'La prière chrétienne et la prière païnne, formes et différences'; Dölger, *Sol Salutis: Gebet und Gesang im christlichen Altertum mit besonderer Rücksicht auf die Ostung in Gebet und Liturgie*; Klawek, *Das Gebet zu Jesus. Seine Berechtigung und Übung nach den Schriften des Neuen Testaments: Eine biblische-theologische Studie*; Jungmann, *The Place of Christ in Liturgical Prayer*; Lebreton, *Histoire du dogme de la trinité*, 2: 175–247; Cullmann, *Prayer in the New Testament*.

[26] Bauckham complains, 'The NT evidence for personal prayer to Jesus has sometimes been underestimated', citing the same evidence noted here ('Jesus, Worship of,' 813). For the Pauline evidence, Hamman's analysis is crucial (*La prière*, 245–337). Especially see his discussion of the question of to whom prayer is addressed in Paul, 264–80.

addressed and invoked together (1 Thess. 3:11–13; 2 Thess. 2:16–17; 3:5). To these we should add the characteristic 'Grace and peace' salutation in Paul's letter-openings, which invoke God and Jesus and are probably to be understood as Paul's adaptation of religious expressions and practices used in his churches (Rom. 1:7; 1 Cor. 1:3; 2 Cor. 1:3; Gal. 1:3; Phil. 1:2; 2 Thess. 1:2).[27] Also relevant are the Pauline grace-benedictions that conclude his letters and are likewise reflective of early Christian devotional and liturgical practice, in which Jesus is invoked as source of the grace, most often alone (Rom. 16:20; 1 Cor. 16:23; Gal. 6:18; Phil. 4:23; 1 Thess. 5:28; 2 Thess. 3:18), and once in the triadic expression familiar to many Christians from 2 Corinthians 13:13. These expressions, in letters intended to be read out in the Christian groups to which they were addressed as a part of their worship and reflecting the liturgical expressions characteristic of these groups, show that already well within the first two decades of the Christian movement it was common (and uncontroversial among believers) to include Jesus with God as source of the blessings invoked and appealed for in their devotional life.

In the Pauline letters, direct, personal prayer to Jesus is explicit only in 2 Corinthians 12:8–9, where Paul mentions repeated appeals to 'the Lord' to remove an affliction sent from Satan. It is correct to note that Paul probably refers here to private prayer, and thus this is not a formal, corporate prayer-text. But Paul's easy recounting of his actions suggests that he expects his readers to be familiar with prayer-appeals to Jesus as a communally accepted feature of Christian devotional praxis.

The account of Stephen's death, though found in a writing most would date later than Paul's letters, gives us another instance of direct prayer to Jesus (Acts 7:59–60). This is also a personal prayer, but again it seems likely that the author expects his Christian readers to be quite familiar with Jesus as

---

[27] E.g., J. L. White, 'New Testament Epistolary Literature in the Framework of Ancient Epistolography' in Temporini and Haase (eds.) *Aufstieg und Niedergang der römischen Welt.*

recipient of prayers.[28] Direct prayer to Jesus is in fact much more common in the apocryphal Christian literature. As these writings are often taken as reflective of 'popular' Christian piety rather than more tutored and 'official' practice, it may be that direct prayer to Jesus was more common in popular Christian practice, even in the earliest period of the Christian movement, than is explicitly evidenced in the New Testament.[29] The reference in Acts 13:2 to the disciples in Antioch 'worshipping the Lord' (*leitourgounton de auton to kyrio*), though slightly ambiguous, quite plausibly has the exalted Jesus as the referent.[30]

2. Invocation and Confession

Whatever the frequency and prominence of prayers addressed to Jesus in Christian corporate worship, either directly or with God, it is fairly clear that there were also other ritual acts of corporate worship in which Jesus is the one addressed and invoked, and that these practices go back to the earliest decades of the Christian movement. For chronological purposes, the well-known fragment of Christian Aramaic liturgical usage preserved in transliterated Greek in 1 Corinthians 16:22, *maranatha*, takes pride of place.[31] It is usually

---

[28] Lebreton (*Dogme de la trinité*, 226–38) draws attention to a pattern of direct prayer to Christ in accounts of Christian martyrdom, of which the Stephen account is earliest and for which it may have been paradigmatic. The connection of prayer to Jesus and accounts of Christian martyrs is noted also by Bauckham ('Jesus, Worship of,' 817).

[29] On prayer to Jesus in Christian apocryphal literature, see Jungmann, *Liturgical Prayer*, 165–68.

[30] The expression appears frequently in the Greek Bible where it clearly carries a cultic sense: e.g., 1 Sam. 3:1; 2 Chron. 11:14; 35:3; Joel 1:13; 2:17; *Judith* 4:14; *Sir.* 7:30; 45:15.

[31] See my discussion in *One God, One Lord* (106–7); Conzelmann, *1 Corinthians*, 300–1; Fee, *The First Epistle to the Corinthians*, 837–39; and now also Davis, *The Name and Way of the Lord: Old Testament Themes, New Testament Christology*, 136–39, whose concluding judgements, however, seem to me too weak.

understood as an imperative appeal, to be translated, 'Our Lord, come!', an appeal or acclamation that arose in the worship gatherings of Aramaic-speaking Christians. By the date of 1 Corinthians (ca. 55 CE) it had become such a familiar liturgical expression as to require no translation, even among Paul's Greek-speaking Gentile converts.[32] The precise function of the expression in its original provenance is disputed, but the consensus now is that in this fragment of the liturgical practices of the earliest decades Jesus is addressed ritually (and probably collectively) as the 'Lord'. Whether he is invoked to be present at the cultic event or (as is more commonly thought now) is implored to come eschatologically, such an appeal to Jesus as a feature of earliest Christian worship has no known parallel in any other group linked to the Jewish religious matrix, and this ritual practice evidences an incorporation of Jesus into the corporate devotional life of those Christians in a role that is otherwise reserved for God.[33] It is not merely that Jesus is now 'the Lord' who is expected to come to make all things right, playing the role attributed to God in Jewish expectation (e.g., *1 Enoch* 1:9). Even more striking is the apparent modification of otherwise known monotheistic liturgical practice in this ritual invocation of Jesus.

From Paul's letters onward, we find other references to ritual acts directed toward Jesus by name. Among these references, Romans 10:9-13 is particularly worth attention. Here, Paul mentions confessing (*homologeo*) 'Jesus (is) Lord' (*Kyrios Iesous*, v. 9) along with belief in Jesus' resurrection as the standard actions through which one comes to eschatological salvation.[34] As is well known, basically the same confession

---

[32] Of course, as is well known, the formula also appears untranslated in Didache 10:6, as part of the eucharistic prayer prescribed there.

[33] On the eschatological background of the phrase, which shows the transference to Jesus of expectation originally directed to God, see Black, 'The Maranatha Invocation and Jude 14, 15 (1 Enoch 1:9)' in Lindars and Smalley (eds.), *Christ and Spirit in the New Testament*, 189-96.

[34] Neufeld, *The Earliest Christian Confessions*, 42-68.

is attested in 1 Corinthians 12:3, where it is directly connected to the impulse of the Holy Spirit in a context clearly concerned with liturgical matters (1 Cor. 12–14), and in Philippians 2:11, where it is the eschatological acclamation of all creation, in a passage commonly thought to derive from the liturgical practices of the earliest Christian decades.

The linguistic and semantic background and implications of the *kyrios* title have been abundantly explored and debated by scholars, but I emphasise here the liturgical setting and function of the formula. In each case in these Pauline references, the setting of the expressions is the Christian congregation and collective worship.[35] Cf. Neufeld, *Christian Confessions*, 60–67, who unpersuasively tries to link the confession-act too narrowly to situations of trial, conflict and persecution. This makes the (probably collective) action of confessing Jesus as Lord itself a liturgical act that functioned ritually to affirm the nature of the group as gathered under Jesus' authority and efficacy. Indeed, this liturgical acclamation of Jesus' present exaltation and eschatological triumph seems to have been intended to enact his triumph ritually within the Christian assembly.

In fact, Paul and other New Testament authors can refer to Christians as those who ritually 'call upon' (*epikaloumai*) Jesus as Lord, which indicates that the liturgical action connoted by this expression was early seen as constitutive and denotative of Christian devotional life.[36] Coming shortly after the reference to the crucial confession of Jesus as 'Lord' as the means to salvation in Romans 10:9, Paul's quotation of Joel 2:32, 'Everyone who calls upon the name of the Lord shall be saved', can only be taken as referring to the ritual invocation of Jesus. Indeed, in 1 Corinthians 1:2b, Paul specifies Jesus by name as the Lord who is invoked and makes the cultic action in question the

---

[35] Cf. Neufeld, *Christian Confessions*, 60–67, who unpersuasively tries to link the confession-act too narrowly to situations of trial, conflict and persecution.

[36] See my earlier discussion in *One God, One Lord*, 108–11. On the OT background of this phrase and action, and the NT references to it, see Davis, *Name and Way*, 103–40.

blanket description of believers (see also, e.g., Acts 9:14, 21; 22:16; 2 Tim. 2:22). In the Old Testament, to 'call upon the name of the LORD' (in the LXX rendered consistently by the middle forms of *epikaleo*) is a ritual action of worship.[37] It is quite likely that 'calling upon the name of the Lord Jesus' includes specifically the liturgical 'confession' of Jesus as Lord.[38] But, in light of the Old Testament background of the expression, I suggest that 'calling upon the name of the Lord (Jesus)' connoted the broader praxis of treating the exalted Jesus as recipient of the devotion of the Christian community through invocation, prayer and praise. The adoption of this Old Testament phrase, which there refers to cultic devotion to God, to designate cultic devotion to Jesus is a striking linguistic appropriation. But the phenomenon to which the phrase refers, the incorporation of Jesus as recipient of organised cultic devotion in early Christian congregations, is an even more daring and remarkable development.[39] Indeed, the adoption/adaptation of the Old Testament cultic expression to connote devotion to Jesus is probably to be seen as indicating that these early Christians intended a direct association and analogy between their devotion to Jesus and the Old Testament cultic devotion to *Yahweh*.

This direct association of Jesus with God in the cultic life of early Christian congregations is powerfully illustrated in 1 Corinthians 5:1–5, where Paul orders the Corinthian congregation to discipline a man who was living sexually with 'his father's wife'. The corporate judgement against the man is to be taken in the cultic (worship) setting. Gathered 'in the name of the Lord Jesus' and with 'the power of our Lord Jesus', the congregation is to deliver the offender to Satan, apparently in the hope that the man might be saved on 'the day of the

---

[37] *Ibid.*, 103–10; Schmidt, 'ἐπικαλεω', in Kittel and Friedrich (eds.), *Theological Dictionary*, 496–500.

[38] Kramer (*Christ, Lord, Son of God*, 79) argued that the Christian appropriation of the expression originally referred to cultic confession and then spread to other ritual actions. See also Vielhauer, *Aufsätze zum Neuen Testament*, 141–98.

[39] Hurtado, *One God, One Lord*, 109, 165 n. 58.

Lord'.[40] Jesus is the eschatological Lord whose coming is here referred to with the Old Testament expression for God's salvific appearance, a remarkable linkage of Jesus with functions of God.[41] But it is even more remarkable that 'the Lord Jesus' is also the one in whose name and power the cultic gathering takes place and the disciplinary judgement is issued. We must infer the practice of a ritual invoking of Jesus' name to constitute the assembly, and the disciplinary action Paul prescribes likely included a ritual invocation of Jesus' name and power to effect it. Jesus' cultic presence and power clearly operate here in the manner we otherwise associate with a god.[42] Moreover, there is simply no parallel for this in any other group of the period with comparable connections to the biblical/Jewish monotheistic scruple against involving figures other than the God of Israel in cultic devotion. By contrast,

---

[40] I take 'in the name of the Lord Jesus' here as modifying the participial phrase, *synachthentōn hymnōn* agreeing with the translations in the NIV, JB, and NEB, against the RSV, NRSV, CEV, NAB. Cf. Fee, *Corinthians*, 206–8. Even if the phrase is taken as modifying Paul's own verdict, the congregation is still to act 'with the power of our Lord Jesus', which makes this clearly a cultic scene and action in which Jesus is central. On the textual variants in v. 4 (the/our Lord Jesus), see Fee, *Corinthians*, 198. The close association of Jesus' eschatological and present/cultic lordship in this passage also illustrates the fallacy of the notion that these two themes have a separate history and can be fitted into some evolutionary theory. In 'Atonement Texture in 1 Corinthians 5.5', *Journal for the Study of the New Testament* 71, (1998), 29–50, Schillington argues (with some others) that Paul envisions the death of the incestuous man, and that the purpose clause (*hina to pneuma sothe en te hemera tou kyriou*) refers to the preservation of the Holy Spirit in the church, not the spirit of the man. But Schillington's repeated claims of 'allusion' to the scapegoat ritual (in Lev. 16) in the passage have no basis, and he ignores 1 Tim. 1:20, where the author also refers to handing people over to Satan with a disciplinary intention for the offenders. On 1 Cor. 5:1–5, I deem Fee's discussion to be most helpful (*Corinthians*, 199–214).
[41] Kreitzer, *Jesus and God in Paul's Eschatology*.
[42] Cf. the OT accounts of cultic approach to *Yahweh* to maintain community purity/obedience, e.g., Josh. 7:10–26.

note the emphasis in *1 Enoch* on the name of God: denying (45:1; 46:7), glorifying/blessing/extolling (46:6; 48:6; 61:9, 11–12; 63:7), and the elect victorious through God's name (50:2–3). The action Paul prescribes here may not be what one ordinarily thinks of as 'worship', but it is undeniably a cultic setting and action with Jesus' name and power to give it efficacy, and this surely reflects a central place for him in the broader cultic life of these congregations.

The cultic invocation of Jesus' name is probably reflected also in Philippians 2:9–11, where the universal acclamation of Jesus as Lord is to be done 'in/at the name of Jesus' (v. 10; *en to onomati Iesou*). It is commonly granted that the universal acclamation projected in these verses was seen by Christians as an eschatological vindication of the cultic confession of Jesus' lordship already celebrated in early Christian cultic practice. It is also commonly recognised that the 'in/at the name of Jesus' phrase likely derives from Christian cultic rhetoric and practice in which the name of Jesus was ritually invoked to constitute the cultic occasion in which he was also acclaimed as Lord.[43]

3. Baptism

By all accounts, the principal rite through which people became members of early Christian groups was a baptism that involved the invocation of Jesus' name (*epi to onomati Iesou*, e.g., Acts 2:38; *eis to onoma tou kyriou Iesou*, Acts 8:16; *en to onomati Iesou Christou*, Acts 10:48).[44] To make the entrance rite into the elect so directly connected with Jesus is itself notable, for it

---

[43] Deissmann, 'The Name "Jesus" ' in Bell and Deissmann (eds.), *Mysterium Christi: Christological Studies by British and German Theologians*, discusses the historical background of the name 'Jesus'.

[44] It is commonly accepted that the 'trinitarian' baptismal formula of Matt. 28:19 and *Did.* 7:1 (but cf. 9:5!) is probably a somewhat later expression and that earliest practice is the 'in/into the name of Jesus' formula; Heitmüller, *'Im Name Jesu'*: *Eine sprach-und-religionsgeschichtlich Untersuchung zum Neuen Testament, speziell zur altchristlichen Taufe*; Hartman, 'Baptism "into the name of Jesus" and Early Christology: Some Tentative Considerations',

reflects belief in Jesus as the living guarantor of the salvation promised to those who trust in him. This ritual invocation of Jesus' name over the baptised has no parallel in other Jewish proselyte practice or in the entrance rites of groups such as the Qumran sect, and it is surely another strong indication of the re-shaping of monotheistic cultic practice that was characteristic of early Christian circles. Moreover, as Hartman has noted, the use of the title *Kyrios* in the formula of this cultic action must mean that Jesus is regarded in ways analogous to the ways God is regarded, and the baptismal use of this title for Jesus is itself good evidence that in such uses it carries the force of a divine title.[45]

This ritual invocation of Jesus is reflected in Paul's references to being baptised 'into [*eis*] Christ (Jesus)' (Rom. 6:3; Gal. 3:27), and also in Paul's reminder to the Corinthians that they had certainly not been baptised in (*eis*) his own name (1 Cor. 1:15).[46] The pronouncing of Jesus' name in baptism must have functioned as a ritual means of bringing to bear upon the baptised the power of the exalted Jesus, and it marked the person as the property of Jesus (e. g., 1 Cor. 1:12; 3:23; Gal. 3:29).[47] This is why Paul can describe the baptised as having 'put on Christ'

[44] *(continued)* Studia Theologica 28 (1974), 21–48; *id.*, ' "Into the Name of Jesus" ', *New Testament Studies* 20 (1974), 432–40.; *id.*, 'Baptism', in Freedman, D. N. (ed.), *Anchor Bible Dictionary*; *id.*, '*Into the Name of the Lord Jesus': Baptism in the Early Church*; Beasley-Murray, *Baptism in the New Testament*.

[45] Hartman, 'Early Baptism-Early Christology' in Malherbe and Meeks (eds.) *The Future of Christology: Essays in Honor of Leander E. Keck*, 197.

[46] Paul's reference to 'our ancestors' being 'baptised into Moses in the cloud and in the sea', like the references to the Israelites consuming 'spiritual food' and 'spiritual drink' (1 Cor. 10:1–5), is simply a case of retroactively applying the cultic rituals and language of his congregations to the OT narratives as part of his larger hortatory purpose in the wider context. There is certainly no evidence that conversion to Judaism involved a ritual invocation of Moses. On this passage see, e.g., Fee, *Corinthians*, 443–48; Beasley-Murray, *Baptism*, 181–85.

[47] Hartman, 'Baptism' shows the legal background of the 'in the name' formula.

(Gal. 3:27), and as having been 'buried with him [Christ] into his death' through the rite (Rom. 6:4).

Though questions of the influence of pagan cults upon earliest Christian practice and thought involve more complex analysis than can be given here, it is clear that there are certain phenomenological analogies between the significance and role of Jesus in early Christian baptism and the significance and role of the deities of pagan mysteries. As in the pagan rites, in which initiates were assured of the power of the deity into whose rites they were entering, so early Christian baptism seems to have involved coming under the power of Jesus as the divinely-appointed Lord.[48] Thus, baptism, with Jesus' name operating as the efficacious power invoked, is another major feature of the devotional pattern of earliest Christian groups.

4. The 'Lord's Supper'[49]

It is not necessary here to engage questions about the form of the meal and the possible evolution of sacred-meal practices and formulae in early Christian groups.[50] It is commonly

---

[48] See, e.g., Wedderburn, *Baptism and Resurrection: Studies in Pauline Theology against its Graeco-Roman Background*, esp. 331, 357–58.

[49] Most recently, Klauck, 'Lord's Supper', in Freedman, D. N. (ed.), *Anchor Bible Dictionary*; id., *Herrenmahl und hellenistischer Kult*. Accessible discussions of issues are given in Marshall, *Last Supper and Lord's Supper*, and also in Kodell, *The Eucharist in the New Testament*.

[50] E.g., the classic theory of Lietzmann, *Mass and Lord's Supper: A Study in the History of the Liturgy*. Kodell (*Eucharist*, 22–37) gives a helpful overview of recent scholarship. Marxsen's detailed theses about the evolution of earliest Lord's Supper practice depend too much on simplistic notions of 'Palestinian' and 'Hellenistic' spheres of early Christianity and on the unexamined assumption of a unilinear process (*The Beginnings of Christology Together with The Lord's Supper as a Christological Problem*). On the use of the words of institution from the Last Supper narratives in early eucharistic practice, see McGowan, ' "Is There a Liturgical Text in this Gospel?" The Institution Narratives and their Early Interpretive Communities', *Journal of Biblical Literature* 118 (1999), 73–87.

accepted that a sacred meal, among other things signifying in some way the religious fellowship of participants, was characteristic of Christian groups from the earliest years onward. The earliest references are in 1 Corinthians 11:17–34, where Paul corrects certain misbehaviour in the context of the sacred meal, and in 10:14–22, where the Christian sacred meal is both compared and contrasted with the cult meals of the pagan gods of Corinth. For my purposes, the main question is what sort of connection there is between this Christian cultic meal and the exalted Jesus.

First, whatever the specific meal practices and formulae, the frequency of the meal (e.g., daily or weekly), and the explicit religious emphases attached to it by various early Christian groups (e.g., an eschatological emphasis, a connection with the death/sacrifice of Jesus, etc.), it is appropriate to refer to the Christian fellowship meal as a 'cultic' occasion, that is, a formal worship occasion that formed part of their devotional pattern. A common meal specifically expressive of their Christian fellowship was clearly an important feature of the congregational life of early Christian groups, and was equally clearly much more than simply a conveniently scheduled eating time. In Paul's references to the meal in 1 Corinthians, there are profound religious themes attached to the rite, and these appear to have already become traditional by the 50s of the first century (that is, within the first two decades of the Christian movement).

Paul refers to the meal as the 'Lord's Supper' (*kyriakon deipnon*, 1 Cor. 11:20), which directly associates the meal with Jesus as the Lord of the Christian congregation.[51] In

---

[51] Outside of Christian usage for the 'Lord's Supper' and the 'Lord's Day', the term *kyriakos* is used in the Roman period with reference to Roman imperial matters and items, as noted in Chapter 2 and as shown long ago by Deissmann (*Bible Studies*, 217–19; and *id.*, *Light From the Ancient East*, 357–60); and see *MM* 364. We cannot here engage Deissmann's thesis that the term was deliberately taken over by Paul for the Christian meal as expressive of a political stance critical of the claims of the Roman emperor. Cf. Foerster, 'κυριακός', in Kittel and Friedrich (eds.), *Theological Dictionary*.

1 Corinthians 11:27 and 10:21, he refers to the 'cup of the Lord' (*poterion kyriou*) and 'the table of the Lord' (*trapezes kyriou*), which reflects the same direct association. In 11:23–26, Paul recites what he connects with tradition given to him 'from the Lord', which is commonly taken to mean that Paul was taught these traditions by the sort of people he else-where refers to as 'those who were in Christ before me' (Rom. 16:7).[52] According to this tradition, the bread and wine are directly associated with Jesus' redemptive death (11:24–25), which in fact is made constitutive of 'the new covenant' (v. 25); and Paul makes the continuing cult-meal practice a proclamation of the death of 'the Lord' until his eschatological return (v. 26).

In his handling of the question of Christian participation in the cult meals of the pagan gods (1 Cor. 10:14–22), Paul directly poses as exclusive alternatives such feasts and the Christian cultic meal. He makes the cup and bread a 'fellow-ship' (*koinonia*) in the blood and body of Christ (v. 16), and draws a direct analogy between this cultic fellowship and the fellowship of those who jointly partook of sacrificial meals in the Jerusalem Temple (v. 18). In language influenced by the Old Testament, Paul refers here to the danger of 'provoking the Lord to jealousy' (v. 22), which powerfully illustrates the cultic place of Jesus as the Lord whose divine power is to be reckoned with, as reflected also in 11:29–32, where Paul warns of the serious consequences of being judged by 'the Lord' for inappropriate behaviour at the cultic meal.

In short, the cult-meal of the Christian congregation is here emphatically one in which the Lord Jesus plays a role that is explicitly likened to that of the deities of the pagan cults and of God![53] This is not merely a memorial feast for a dead hero. Jesus is portrayed as the living power who owns the meal and presides at it, and with whom believers have fellowship as with a god.

---

[52] E. g., Hunter, *Paul and His Predecessors*.
[53] Klauck, 'Presence in the Lord's Supper: 1 Corinthians 11:23–26 in the Context of Hellenistic Religious History'.

Once again, I know of no analogy for such a cultic role for any figure other than God in Jewish religious circles of the Second Temple period. As I emphasised in *One God, One Lord*, in the cultic/sacred meals of other Jewish groups such as the Qumran sect, none of the figures so prominent in their eschatological outlook (e.g., the Teacher of Righteousness, Priest, royal Messiah, Melchizedek) has any place comparable to Jesus in the sacred meal of early Christian groups.[54]

5. *Hymns*[55]

Several NT passages indicate the prominent place of songs in the devotional life of early Christianity (e.g., 1 Cor. 14:26; Col. 3:16–17; Eph. 5:18–20; James 5:14; Acts 16:25), and scholars commonly see a number of NT passages as incorporating

---

[54] Hurtado, *One God, One Lord*, 111–12. See K. G. Kuhn, 'The Lord's Supper and the Communal Meal at Qumran' in Stendahl (ed.), *The Scrolls and the New Testament*, 65–93, esp. 77–78.

[55] Deichgräber, *Gotteshymnus und Christushymnus in der frühen Christenheit*; Schille, *Frühchristliche Hymnen*; Wengst, *Christologische Formeln und Lieder des Urchristenum*; Kennel, *Frühchristliche Hymnen? Gattungskritische Studien zur Frage nach den Leidern der frühen Christenheit*; Kroll, *Die christliche Hymnodik bis zu Klemens von Alexandreia*; J. T. Sanders, *The New Testament Christological Hymns: Their Historical Religious Background*; Thompson, 'Hymns in Early Christian Worship', *Anglican Theological Review* 55 (1973), 458–72; W. S. Smith, *Musical Aspects of the New Testament*; McKinnon, *Music in Early Christian Literature*. In several publications, Martin Hengel has emphasised the importance of hymns as a mode of earliest christological affirmation: 'Hymns and Christology' in Hengel, *Between Jesus and Paul*; id., 'The Song about Christ in Earliest Worship' in Hengel, *Studies in Early Christology*. See also R. P. Martin, 'Some Reflections on New Testament Hymns' in Rowdon (ed.), *Christ the Lord: Studies Presented to Donald Guthrie*. For the wider background, see Lattke, *Hymnus: Materialien zu einer Geschichte der antiken Hymnologie*; Quasten, *Musik und Gesang in den Kulten der heidnischen Antike und christlichen Frühzeit*; Guthrie, 'Hymns' in Hammond and Scullard (eds.), *The Oxford Classical Dictionary*; Grözinger, *Musik und Gesang in der Theologie der frühen jüdischen Literatur*.

hymnic material from the worship life of first-century Christian circles (e.g., Phil. 2:6–11; Col. 1:15–20; John 1:1–18; Eph. 5:14; 1 Tim. 3:16).[56] The voluminous scholarship on this material has mainly been concerned with the contents, the christological ideas and beliefs reflected in these passages. A few studies have focused on the formal characteristics of these hymns, and a good deal of effort has been expended on trying to determine whether they were all originally composed in Greek or might, in some cases, have originated in Aramaic. The putative hymn in Philippians 2:6–11 has perhaps attracted more attention than any of the other passages, and the work on this passage illustrates the foci I have mentioned here.[57] My emphasis here, however, is on christological hymns/songs as a feature of devotional practice. I examine the phenomenon of singing such christological hymns as a component of the cultic practices of earliest Christian groups, and thereby an important feature of the binitarian worship pattern in which Jesus figures so very prominently.[58]

As Deichgräber pointed out, the New Testament hymnic material is heavily concerned with the celebration of the significance and work of Jesus, with far more of this material concerned with Jesus than with God.[59] From this, one gains the impression that singing/chanting songs in honour of Jesus was not an occasional but a characteristic feature of early Christian worship.[60] This is, of course, precisely the impression of

---

[56] Cabaniss' assertion that there was no singing in earliest Christian worship is bizarre (*Pattern in Early Christian Worship*, 50–51, 53).

[57] Martin, *Carmen Christi: Philippians 2:5–11 in Recent Interpretation and in the Setting of Early Christian Worship*. In the second edition of this book, Martin updates the review of scholarly discussion of the passage.

[58] Hurtado, *One God, One Lord*, 101–4.

[59] Deichgräber, *Gotteshymnus und Christushymnus*, 60–61, 207–8.

[60] It is not easily possible to say exactly what musical mode was involved, but unaccompanied 'chanting' or musical cantilisation was likely frequent. On the terms used and evidence of the 'manner of musical performance', see W. S. Smith, *Musical Aspects of the New Testament*, esp. 22–27.

early Christian worship given in Pliny's well-known letter to Trajan (111–112 CE), which refers to the practice of antiphonal singing 'to Christ as to their God' (*carmenque Cristo quasi deo*); the 'singing' here is probably to be taken as unaccompanied chanting.[61] Christological singing is referred to also in letters of Ignatius of Antioch (*Ign.Eph.* 4:1–2; *Ign.Rom.* 2:2), approximately contemporary with Pliny.

One should also note that, in addition to the hymnic material in the New Testament and other early Christian sources, it is most likely that a great part of earliest Christian 'hymnody' involved the chanting of Old Testament psalms, interpreted christologically.[62] Indeed, the influence of Psalm 110 and other psalms reflected in the New Testament is probably to be accounted for by positing their familiarity through wide and frequent usage in earliest Christian worship.[63] I suggest that in the setting of early Christian worship, in which the Spirit was expected to inspire believers and bestow revelations, the Old Testament psalms, especially those that had already begun to be read as royal-messianic psalms in some pre-Christian Jewish circles, were 'unlocked' as predictions of Jesus and as descriptions of his glory. As Christians were 'enlightened' to understand the Psalms christologically, they were chanted as praise of Jesus, and likely became a familiar feature of earliest

---

[61] Pliny, *Epistles* 10.96.7. Commentary by Sherwin-White, *The Letters of Pliny*, 691–710. Tertullian (*Apology* 2.6) and Eusebius (*HE* 3.33.1) cite Pliny's statement and show that they understood it to refer to hymns sung about and to Christ as to a god. Cf. Hengel, 'The Song about Christ', 263. Note *2 Clem.* 1:1, 'Brothers, we ought to think of Jesus Christ, as we do of God . . .' [*phronein peri Iesou Christou hos peri Theou*].

[62] Thus, e.g., Hengel, 'The Song about Christ', 258–60; Old, 'The Psalms of Praise in the Worship of the New Testament Church' *Interpretation* 39 (1985), 20–33.

[63] Hay, *Glory at the Right Hand: Psalm 110 in Early Christianity*; Juel, *Messianic Exegesis: Christological Interpretation of the Old Testament in Early Christianity*. Of the many studies of the NT interpretation of the OT, I know of none that places much emphasis on the worship setting as the place where and how OT texts first became meaningful christologically.

worship (e.g., 1 Cor. 14:26; Col. 3:16; Eph. 5:19). The 'exegesis' of these crucially important Old Testament passages was not in a seminar, discussion group or at a desk, but emerged initially in inspired insights coming in the exalted context of pneumatic worship. Along with this christological interpretation/appropriation of OT psalms, there were also fresh compositions pneumatically inspired and patterned after the biblical psalms (e.g., Luke 1:46–55; 67–79; 2:29–32; Phil. 2:6–11; the heavenly hymns of Rev. 4:11; 5:9–10), just as there were among the Qumran sect (e.g., *1QH*; extra-canonical in psalms scrolls such as *11QPs*).[64] It is difficult, in fact, to tell whether the 'psalm' referred to in the New Testament passages as a characteristic feature of Christian worship is to be taken as one of these or as something from the Old Testament collection. Perhaps both types are included, as the use of both would have emerged from the inspiration of the Spirit, either as revelations of the meaning of Old Testament material or as newly minted praise.

The christological focus of much/most of earliest Christian hymnody is undeniable, and it is also distinctive in comparison with any evidence we have of Jewish religious groups of the period.[65] To be sure, in the OT Psalter there are psalms in praise of the king (e.g., Pss. 2; 42; 110) which would have been chanted in Jewish worship settings, and among the extra-canonical material of the time there are compositions that concerned a messianic figure and that may have been used liturgically by the groups among which these compositions originated (e.g., *Psalms of Solomon* 17–18).[66] But there is

---

[64] For English translations of these and other Qumran texts, see, e.g., Martínez, *The Dead Sea Scrolls Translated: The Qumran Texts in English*. For *1QH*, pp. 317–70; for *11QPs*, pp. 304–10.

[65] Flusser, 'Psalms, Hymns and Prayers' in M. E. Stone (ed.), *Jewish Writings of the Second Temple Period*; Charlesworth, 'Jewish Hymns, Odes, and Prayers (ca. 167 B.C.E.–135 C.E.)' in Kraft and Nickelsburg (eds.), *Early Judaism and its Modern Interpreters*.

[66] For an English translation of *Psalms of Solomon* (and a number of other extra-canonical texts), see Sparks, *The Apocryphal Old Testament*, or Charlesworth, *Pseudepigrapha*.

nothing like the concentration on the figure of Jesus that characterised early Christian liturgical song. Thus, at the very least, we have to grant a major degree of difference from the liturgical practices and pattern more characteristic of Jewish groups.

Moreover, although early Christians were strongly resistant to charges that they worshipped two gods and that their devotion to Jesus constituted any threat to their monotheistic commitment (as I shall emphasise in the final section of this chapter), their powerful sense of Jesus' exalted power and his relationship to them as Lord profoundly shaped what they did and how they understood it. Thus, for example, we have references to their worship and praise as offered *to God* and *in the name of Jesus* and *through* Jesus (e.g., Col. 3:16–17). That is, Jesus is very often the content and occasion for worship and liturgical song or chant, and is also characteristically the one through whom the worship and praise is efficacious.

In some New Testament passages we even have indications of hymns sung *to* Jesus.[67] Ephesians 5:19 prescribes singing 'to the Lord', who is likely the exalted Jesus (cf. 'to God' in the Col. 3:16 parallel), and in Revelation we have praise and worship, including hymnic praise, directed jointly to God and 'the Lamb' (5:8–10, 13–14; 7:9–12). These scenes of heavenly worship are certainly idealised and we cannot take them to be direct reflections of liturgical practices of the churches in Asia Minor to which the prophet John writes; but it is likely that the themes and general understanding of worship in these heavenly scenes are influenced by the worship of the author's earthly experience.[68] Thus it is reasonable to infer that in the author's experience cultic praise concerned Jesus and God and was seen as directed to both.

J. D. G. Dunn implies that these references to praise directed to Jesus indicate that Christians of the post-Pauline

---

[67] Hurtado, *One God, One Lord*, 102–3.

[68] Mowry 'Revelation 4–5 and Early Christian Liturgical Usage', *Journal of Biblical Literature* 71 (1952), 75–84; Piper, 'The Apocalypse of John and the Liturgy of the Ancient Church', *Church History* 20 (1951), 10–22.

period lost sight of the greater 'reserve' about worship of Jesus that Dunn attributes to Paul. Dunn also refers to 'a steady transition in worship' in these early Christian circles, a development that he is not sure that Paul would have approved had he been conscious of it.[69] In the final section of this chapter I shall return to the question of how early Christians saw their Christ-devotion in the context of their commitment to the one God. I will anticipate that discussion here briefly to indicate that I do not think that the 'more carefully nuanced formulation in speaking about the cultic veneration of Jesus in earliest Christianity' for which Dunn calls is really advanced by his own comments.[70]

For Dunn to attribute to Paul a 'reserve' suggests that Paul considered direct praise of Jesus and withdrew from it or opposed it. Dunn's reference to a 'transition' implies that we can see a movement from one worship practice to another. In my view, however, neither notion has any basis in the evidence. Given the intensity of devotion to Jesus characteristically reflected in Paul (e.g., Phil. 3:7–16; 2 Cor. 3:12–4:6), it is dubious to attribute to Paul any 'reserve' about Jesus. Paul's references to prayer and worship as directed to God through Jesus and in Jesus' name amount to an unprecedented 'mutation' in the devotional language and practice otherwise attested among devout Jews of the first century. There is no indication in Paul's letters that among the problems he ever had to deal with was anxiety about devotion

---

[69] Dunn, *Theology of Paul*, 260.

[70] Ibid., 260. The 'ancient distinction between "worship" and "veneration" ' to which Dunn refers is not nearly ancient enough to be relevant for NT exegesis. The technical distinctions between 'latria' (reverence for God), 'hyperdulia' (reverence for the Virgin Mary), and 'dulia' (reverence for the saints) in Orthodox and Roman Catholic theology arose in response to what were regarded as abuses of the veneration of saints in the fifth century CE! See, e. g., articles on 'Latria', 'Dulia', 'Hyperdulia', and 'Saints, Devotion to the,' in Cross and Livingstone. Cf. *Mart.Pol.* 17:2–3 and the strong second-century distinction between the worship of Jesus and love and respect for the martyrs.

to Jesus representing a possible neglect of God or threat to God's centrality. The final line of the 'hymnic' passage in Philippians 2:6–11 makes the future universal acclamation redound to God's glory (v. 11b) in order to legitimate the acclamation and to give it meaning within the context of the biblical tradition. To be sure, as Dunn notes,[71] Paul's linkage of the acclamation of Jesus with the glory of God can be taken justifiably to forbid the idea that the acclamation of Jesus involves a displacement of God. But there is no reason to think that Paul was aware of any such inference and was seeking to forestall it.

Moreover, it would be dubious to take the praises sung to God and the Lamb in Revelation as indicative of some significant 'transition' in early Christian worship. The author of Revelation shows a sternly negative attitude toward other Christians who advocated what look like innovations in liturgical practice or in scruples about worship, such as those whom he accuses of 'the teaching of Balaam' (2:14) and the woman prophet whom he names 'Jezebel' (2:20), all of whom he denounces as advocating 'fornication and eating food sacrificed to idols'. Throughout Revelation, the author warns about worship of 'the beast' (9:20; 13:4, 8, 12, 15; 14:9, 11; 16:2; 19:20; 20:4), and calls for worship of God alone (14:7; 19:10; 22:9). In the context of the author's strict scruples about worship, the approval he gives to reverence to the Lamb is remarkable, and also without precedent in the Jewish background. But the author's very conservative attitude about worship makes it likely that his portrayal of worship as directed to God *and to Jesus* reflected traditional attitudes and understanding. Furthermore, the traditions with which this Jewish-Christian prophet was acquainted likely included the practices of Jewish-Christian groups, which suggests that in such circles as well as in Gentile-Christian groups cultic reverence was offered both to God and to Jesus, and that reverence offered to Jesus was understood as an extension and expression of reverence for God.

---

[71] Dunn, *Theology of Paul*, 251–52.

6. Prophecy[72]

Prophetic speech, that is, oracles delivered as revelatory speech, was another common feature of earliest Christian worship assemblies. Paul lists prophecy as one of the Spirit-phenomena given to Christians (1 Cor. 12:10; Rom. 12:8; reflected also in Eph. 4:11), and his extended treatment of prophecy in comparison with tongues-speaking in 1 Corinthians 14 indicates that he considers this form of congregational contribution particularly valuable (esp. 14:1–5, 24–25, 31). The essential character of prophecy is the claim to be speaking under direct divine inspiration, the oracle being the words of the deity. Hence the common OT prophetic formula, '(thus) says the LORD'.

For our purposes it is important to note that early Christian prophecy, which was expected to be delivered in the context of the worship assembly, seems to have included oracles presented as inspired by Jesus. In these cases, Jesus was understood to function in the capacity attributed to God or God's Spirit in the Old Testament and subsequent Jewish tradition, as the one whose words are spoken by the prophet.[73] David Aune identified nineteen oracles in the NT in which Jesus is either pictured as the speaker or identified as the source or authority of the prophetic speech, and he found nine more prophetic speeches of Jesus in the early Christian collection of hymns known as *The Odes of Solomon*.[74] The messages of

---

[72] Hill, *New Testament Prophecy*; Aune, *Prophecy in Early Christianity and the Ancient Mediterranean World*; Boring, 'Prophecy (Early Christian)', in Freedman, D. N. (ed.), *Anchor Bible Dictionary*.

[73] Lindblom, *Prophecy in Ancient Israel*; Aune, *Prophecy*, 81–152; Schmitt, 'Prophecy (Pre-exilic Hebrew)', in Freedman, D. N. (ed.), *Anchor Bible Dictionary*; Barton, 'Prophecy (Postexilic Hebrew)', in Freedman, D. N. (ed.), *Anchor Bible Dictionary*.

[74] Aune, *Prophecy in Early Christianity*, 328–29. The New Testament texts he cites include the seven oracles to the churches in Rev. 2–3; Rev. 16:15; 22:12–15, 16, 20; 2 Cor. 12:9; Acts 18:19; 23:11; 1 Thess. 4:15–17; 1 Cor. 14:37–38; 1 Thess. 4:2; 2 Thess. 3:6, 12.

Jesus to the seven churches in Revelation 2 and 3 are also attributed to the Spirit (cf. 2:1, 7, 8, 11, 12, 17, 18, 29; 3:1, 6, 7, 13, 14, 22), just as Old Testament prophecy can be linked both to Yahweh and the Spirit. This confirms the sense of the exalted Jesus functioning in New Testament prophecy very similarly to God. In addition to those texts cited by Aune, we might note Acts 9:10–17, which narrates Jesus' summoning of Ananias in a visionary oracle to welcome Saul of Tarsus as a fellow believer. Whatever the historicity of the narrative, the mere fact that Jesus is represented in this way is indicative that in early Christian circles prophecy could be experienced as the voice of the exalted Jesus.

There is strong Pauline evidence for Jesus being linked directly with the phenomenon of Christian prophecy. Several passages appear to be prophetic words from the exalted Jesus. In 2 Corinthians 12:9 Paul quotes such an oracle as given to him personally. It is widely thought that 1 Thessalonians 4:15–17 is to be taken as giving (or based on) a prophetic oracle of the risen Jesus, and Aune gives reasons to see 1 Thessalonians 4:2 and 2 Thessalonians 3:6, 12 as examples of the same phenomenon. In 1 Corinthians 14:37–38, Paul appears to claim such prophetic authority for the teaching he has given on behaviour in the worship assembly.

Given the concern in the OT about false prophecy (e.g., Deut. 13:1–5), and the lack of any parallel examples of prophetic oracles delivered in first-century Jewish group worship and attributed to other divine-agent figures, this attribution of prophecy to the exalted Jesus is simply extraordinary. The additional point I wish to reiterate here is that early Christian prophecy was often, perhaps characteristically, a feature of the liturgical life of Christian groups. This justifies taking these prophetic oracles of the risen Jesus as another striking feature of the worship pattern of these groups. As the heavenly Lord who addressed them in prophetic authority, and from whom such oracles were likely sought in prayer, Jesus featured in their liturgical/devotional life in a way that indicates a significant development in Jewish monotheistic practice.

The Binitarian Nature of Early Christian Worship

In describing early Christian worship as characteristically 'binitarian', I emphasise that despite the duality (God and Jesus as recipients of devotion), there is also a clearly evident commitment to an exclusivistic monotheism.[75] The early Christian devotional pattern does not express itself as involving two deities, although there are certainly two figures named as recipients of the devotion. As we noted earlier, in the NT prayer, praise and thanksgiving are characteristically described as given to God through Jesus or in Jesus' name. For example, Richardson notes, 'God is always the object of Pauline thanksgivings, but the content is always explicitly or implicitly christological'.[76] We also surely have evidence of direct prayer and appeal to Jesus. Jesus is invoked and appealed to especially as the Lord of the congregation, gathered in his name and thus in his powerful presence; but gathered thus in their larger view to offer true worship to God 'the Father' (e.g., Matt. 18:19–20).

We also noted earlier that the christological focus of the cultic singing (or chanting) of earliest Christian groups, which shows an inclusion of Jesus in the devotional pattern, is accompanied by clear indications that this reverence of Jesus expresses the praise of and obedience to God. Just as the eschatological, universal acclamation of Jesus as Lord is linked with God's exaltation of him and redounds to the glory of God (Phil. 2:9–11), so in other places service to Christ is acceptable to God (Rom. 14:18), following Jesus glorifies God (Rom. 15:6), and through the divine Son of God, Jesus Christ, believers say 'Amen' to the promises of God and to the glory of God (1 Cor. 11:19–20). Jesus is reverenced in the cultic setting and

---

[75] Important studies include Rohde, 'Gottesglaube und Kyriosglaube bei Paulus', *Zeitschrift für die Neutestamentliche Wissenschaft* 22 (1923), 43–57; Thüsing, *Per Christum in Deum: Studien zum Verhältnis von Christozentrik und Theozentrik in den paulinischen Hauptbriefen*; Kreitzer, *Jesus and God*; Richardson, *Paul's Language about God*.

[76] Richardson, *Paul's Language*, 259. E.g., 1 Thess. 2:13; 3:9; Phil. 1:3; 2 Cor. 8:16.

in actions otherwise (and in other Jewish groups) reserved for God. But the reason given as to why Jesus is entitled to such reverence is because God has conferred this status on him. God has put all things in subjection to Jesus, and the outcome of this rule of Jesus is 'that God may be all in all' (1 Cor. 15:20–28). As the 'image' of God, Jesus shares and manifests the glory of God (2 Cor. 3:12–4:4; Col. 1:15–20; Eph. 1:16–23; Heb. 1:1–4; 2:9), and this is how and why he is to be reverenced in such astonishing ways.[77]

Through God's exaltation of him, Jesus is now able to bestow the Holy Spirit (Acts 2:36), the manifestations of which enable various ministries of Jesus the Lord, which are at the same time 'activities' of God (1 Cor. 12:4–6). This is why Paul's letter-salutations bid 'grace and peace' jointly from God and Jesus, and why Paul's letters characteristically feature a thanksgiving to God near the beginning and a grace-benediction from Jesus at their closings. Through his exaltation, Jesus now dispenses such divine blessings.

Moreover, this reverence of Jesus is completely unlike anything we know in the pagan movements of the Roman era. Jesus is not reverenced as a new god or a deified hero. He does not receive his own cultus distinguished from that given to God 'the Father', and he is not approached for particular types of favours or needs, as if he were seen as having his own divine province or sphere of blessings distinguishable from those God can bestow. Even though the Lord's Supper has certain functional analogies with the cult meals of various gods of the Roman era, this cultic fellowship with him at the table is not something unto itself, but is a manifestation and medium of the cultic gathering to him as the God-appointed Lord, and through this Lord to God the Father.[78] Furthermore, the incorporation of Jesus into earliest Christians'

---

[77] 'Für Paulus ist die Zusammenstellung von Gott und Christus durch die Auferstehung hergestellt worden.' ('For Paul the connection of God and Christ is demonstrated through the resurrection.') Rohde, 'Gottesglaube und Kyriosglaube'.

[78] This point was also noted by Rohde, 'Gottesglaube und Kyriosglaube, 56.

devotional life is not accompanied by the open attitude toward reverencing various deities that was characteristic of the Roman era religious environment. Instead, Jesus is incorporated into an exclusivistic pattern of devotion in which there is room for only *one God and one Lord* (e.g., 1 Cor. 8:5–6). So, what we have is a binitarian, exclusivist monotheism, able to accommodate Jesus, but disdainful of any other god or lord as rightful recipient of devotion.[79]

This full cultic reverence which may be described as 'worship' is given to Jesus, not because early Christians felt at liberty to do so, but because they felt required to do so by God. They reverenced Jesus in observance of God's exaltation of him and in obedience to God's revealed will. This conviction is expressed polemically in John 5:23: 'that all may honour the Son just as they honour the Father. Anyone who does not honour the Son does not honour the Father who sent him.' In Paul, too, the inability to recognise Jesus as the Lord who bears the divine image and glory is attributed to 'hardened' minds blinded by 'the god of this world' (2 Cor. 3:14; 4:4).

This suggests strongly that the cultic reverence of Jesus was not an experiment ventured upon by people seeking on their own to 'push the envelope' of liturgical practice, but was the result of profound convictions likely conveyed through powerful religious experiences that struck the recipients as revelations from God.[80] This unusual 'mutation' in monotheistic practice in turn contributed heavily to the subsequent complicated effort to develop a new doctrine of God, which occupied Christians for the next several centuries.[81]

---

[79] Borgen gives a helpful discussion of the specifics of how Jews and Christians negotiated their particularist scruples in Roman city life (' "Yes," "No," "How Far?": The Participation of Jews and Christians in Pagan Cults' in Engberg-Pedersen (ed.), *Paul in His Hellenistic Context*).

[80] Hurtado, *One God, One Lord*, 114–23, esp. 117–22; and *id.*, 'Religious Experience and Religious Innovation in the New Testament', forthcoming (April 2000) in *Journal of Religion*.

[81] On the crucial second century, see Osborn, *The Emergence of Christian Theology*.

Chapter 4

Reflections for Christian Worship Today

In the previous chapters I have addressed some aspects of the historical context in which earliest Christian worship arose and some of the major features of early Christian worship, showing how Christians incorporated Christ along with God into their devotional life as committed monotheists. My own research and publications over the last twenty years or so have concentrated on these sorts of historical questions about the emergence of devotion to Christ in the first two centuries of Christianity.[1] In what follows, however, I sketch some thoughts about how the worship of Christians today can be enriched and informed by what we can learn of the historical origins of this devotion. This is, thus, a bit of a departure from these more historical questions in order to address contemporary 'applied' concerns, and involves my writing as a worshipping Christian.

Although the topic here has to do with Christian worship and will thus be of most direct interest to other Christians, I invite both Christians and others to consider and interact with my discussion. There is nothing 'private' or confidential about

---

[1] General readers will find an introduction to some of the issues addressed in my previous research in Hurtado, 'The Origins of the Worship of Christ', *Themelios* 19/2 (January 1994), 4–8. This article draws heavily upon my book, *One God, One Lord: Early Christian Devotion and Ancient Jewish Monotheism*. The scope and aims of my research programme are sketched in my article, 'Christ-Devotion in the First Two Centuries: Reflections and a Proposal', *Toronto Journal of Theology* 12 (1996), 17–33.

what follows. Having spent eighteen years in a Department of Religion at a major Canadian public university prior to my present post (in which I teach in both a Divinity degree programme and a Religious Studies degree programme), I am very accustomed to students and scholars of various persuasions engaging the beliefs and practices of various religious traditions. It is an interesting, sometimes very demanding, exercise to try to understand the beliefs, practices and rationale of a faith that one does not share, and it is a good test of a scholar to do so sympathetically and with some accuracy. I also think that it is good for religions to conduct their reflections on their beliefs and practices 'out in the open' so to speak, inviting auditors and visitors as well as adherents to listen and respond. In fact, I propose as a good test of clear thinking by religions whether they can present their beliefs and practices with clarity and some cogency to interested non-adherents.[2] One of the most challenging and invigorating discussions I ever had was with two Iranian Muslim graduate students who had come to Christmas dinner and afterwards quite aggressively demanded explanations of Christian beliefs about God and Christ in terms that they could readily understand.

Moreover, in today's closely connected world, and particularly in Western multi-cultural societies, the beliefs and practices of religions are the legitimate concerns of us all, whatever our own stance toward this or that religion or toward religious faiths in general. Religious beliefs and practices can have an impact upon our lives whether we share them or not. Also, it is simply necessary to interact respectfully and

---

[2] Paul's intricate discussion in 1 Corinthians 14:20–25 seems to indicate that 'unbelievers' (*apistoi*) and 'outsiders' (*idiotai*) could be present in early Christian worship gatherings, and he even makes their ability to understand what is said in the worship service the criterion of clarity. In 2 Corinthians 4:1–6, Paul espouses 'the open statement of the truth' to 'everyone in the sight of God' as the mode of his proclamation. Though I am not technically a theologian, I hope I can be permitted to offer the opinion that Christian theology of the last several centuries would have benefitted had it been required to be conducted in a more thorough and genuine dialogue and debate with other religious traditions.

intelligently with people of various faiths, whether we seek to promote our own faith to others, simply desire religious tolerance and understanding, or wish to engage citizens of our own society or people of other cultures in the unavoidable social, economic, ethical and political issues of our time.[3] The secularist assumption that religion would atrophy and become irrelevant has been proven wrong in very powerful ways in our time.[4] Particular religions may wax or wane, but all indications are that we humans are in the main not going to forsake either the concerns that religions reflect and address or our efforts to engage those concerns through various forms of religious faith and practice. Consequently, serious study of religions is important and of broad value in modern societies. This is the rationale for the study of religions as a modern university discipline, and it also forms part of the reason for inviting readers to 'listen in' on the following discussion whether they participate in Christian worship or choose not to do so.[5]

The reflections in the following pages are based on the premise that contemporary Christian worship and thought should attempt some genuinely fiduciary relationship with biblical precedents while also developing in the light of continuing historical factors. In the space available, it is impossible to give a discussion that will be seen as adequate, especially for anyone not inclined to agree with my views or the premises from which they proceed. I hope, however, at least to stimulate the thinking of others, whatever their response to my thoughts. I am also very conscious that I am venturing here into the sort of discourse more customarily (and likely more

---

[3] For an instructive example of sympathetic and critical engagement with other religions by a Christian thinker, I recommend Cragg, *The Christ and the Faiths*.

[4] See, e.g., Casanova, *Public Religions in the Modern World*; Kepel, *The Revenge of God: The Resurgence of Islam, Christianity and Judaism in the Modern World*.

[5] I have developed this point a bit further in my inaugural lecture, 'New Testament Studies at the Turn of the Millennium: Questions for the Discipline', *Scottish Journal of Theology*, forthcoming.

competently) taken up by 'theologians' in the true sense of the word, scholars whose main research commitment lies in addressing the contemporary needs of Christian theological thinking and its practical consequences.[6]

Monotheism and the Worship of Christ

As we noted in the preceding chapter, from its earliest observable stages Christian worship was directed to God through and with the ascended Christ. That is, in their devotional practice, as in their belief, earliest Christians espoused a binitarian form of monotheism. The first matter I want to address, therefore, is the question of how the worship of Jesus by Christians today could be set within the context and perspective of biblical monotheism. This will require some careful thought, just as it always has among thoughtful Christians!

For example, the attempt of the fourth-century teacher, Arius, to accommodate monotheism by distinguishing between the divine nature of Christ and the divine nature of God the Father ultimately proved misguided and unacceptable in the debates of the fourth century, at least in part because it was seen by critics as implying the worship of two gods. Over against the Arians, Athanasius espoused a view of the relationship of God the Father and the Son that involved their sharing one divine nature while also being clearly distinguishable. In taking such a stance, Athanasius was concerned to develop a theological view of God that was both genuinely monotheistic and also allowed for the traditional Christian devotional practice of treating Christ as a recipient of worship along with God, yet did not lead to a confusion of the two. In the process, he articulated a particularly relational and dynamic form of monotheism that insisted that God's unity transcended all human analogies and was not limited to the finite concepts of oneness.[7]

---

[6] I venture here into the sort of discourse more thoroughly taken up by a previous Didsbury lecturer – see Torrance, *Worship, Community, and the Triune God of Grace.*

[7] Pettersen, *Athanasius.* On Athanasius' views of God, see esp. 36–99.

Though much about his reasoning, his use of the Bible, and his tone toward his opponents bears some critical scrutiny, Athanasius' basic points are still worth considering. I think that Athanasius was correct that Christian theology and worship should be required to have some genuinely mutual relationship. This means that debates among theologians about God and christology are not simply about intellectual issues but also have to do with the central devotional practice of Christian churches.

Thus, if, as some urge today, genuine monotheism precludes the deity of Christ, then Christian devotion would have to make a sharp distinction between the reverence given to Christ and that accorded to God.[8] Otherwise, Christians would risk a violation of their professed historic commitment to worshipping only the one true God. But it needs to be said that if such a sharp distinction were made, the whole shape of traditional Christian devotional practice would have to be radically altered. If, on the other hand, Christians are sincere about their monotheistic commitment and yet also feel obliged to continue the historic Christian devotional pattern of according the sort of reverence to Christ that they otherwise reserve for God, then some kind of profound inclusion of Christ with(in) God such as was articulated in Nicene christology (though not necessarily the same articulation) seems required, or at the very least reasonable. In a study of the formation of Christian doctrines in the early centuries, Maurice Wiles observed, 'Any interpretation of the person of the Son had to be one which came to terms with the place given to him in the Christian practice of devotion.'[9] That is, the distinctive (some might say, peculiar) form of monotheism that developed in the early centuries was intended to give a doctrinal rationale for how Christ could be treated as genuinely divine in devotional practice (as had become customary in most Christian circles) within a commitment to one God.

---

[8] E.g., Casey, *From Jewish Prophet to Gentile God*, esp. 162–81.
[9] Maurice Wiles, *The Making of Christian Doctrine: A Study in the Principles of Early Doctrinal Development*, pp. 62–93, quotation p. 74.

But though some Christians have intellectual difficulties with the deity of Christ, there are other problems perhaps even more characteristic of much popular Christian piety down to the present time. Anyone with much experience of untutored Christian devotion can attest that there is often a confusion of Jesus and God (the 'Father'), or a functional di-theism in which God and Jesus are treated as two gods and any effective monotheistic scruple is overlooked (and when you throw in the Holy Spirit, things really get confusing for many!).[10] These things tend to show up more in informal Christian prayers, and are rarely seen in liturgy that is informed by Christian tradition and theology. But Christians of all denominations and liturgical styles can benefit from thinking seriously about the fundamentally monotheistic nature of Christian faith.

Once again, Christians can profit by carefully drawing upon biblical truths and the lessons of the Christian past. The old creeds and formulations, such as the so-called Nicene Creed, bear the marks of the times in which they were written, of course, but they are in fact much richer than is sometimes recognised today. One relevant illustration will have to suffice to make my point: Christians traditionally worship Jesus as really and genuinely divine, just as we think of God as divine. But, in the words of the Nicene Creed which Christian traditions regard as an instructive statement of belief for continuing reflection, Christ is referred to as 'light *from light*, God *from God*'.[11] Observe that in this formulation Christ is not seen as a second god, but as the one unique 'image', 'Son', and 'Word' of the one God, and, as such, the one Lord of Christians, the one who was made Lord by the one Lord God (e.g., Acts 2:36; Phil. 2:9; 1 Cor. 15:20–28).

---

[10] As an example of the confusion, I quote the following portion of a prayer I recently heard in a Christian worship service: 'Heavenly Father, we thank you that you died on the cross for us . . .'! It is not clear whether this prayer reflects a difficulty in absorbing basic Trinitarian teaching on the relationship of God and Christ or a 'Christo-monism' in which Christ has somehow replaced God.

[11] For English translation and commentary, see, e.g., Schaff, *The Creeds of Christendom*, 1:24–29.

A similar concern to avoid di-theism is reflected in the New Testament references to prayer as characteristically offered *to God* and *in the name of or through* Jesus. In Christian tradition, direct prayer to and invocation of Jesus are also deemed quite appropriate, both privately and corporately, as is evidenced a few times in the New Testament (e.g., Acts 7:59; 2 Cor. 12:8). But it has to be noted that in the devotional tradition represented in the New Testament and classical liturgical practices, any direct prayer or appeal to Christ is always to be framed by the sovereignty of the one God, and is in fact very limited in scope and frequency.[12]

Accordingly, when we Christians properly acclaim Jesus as the one unique *Kyrios* (Lord), we do so '*to the glory of God the Father*' (Phil. 2:9–11), and not apart from or in neglect of the glory of the one God and the monotheistic concern reflected in this Pauline phrase. In the traditional patterns of Eucharist prayer, Christians offer thanksgiving to God for God's Son, Jesus Christ, with whom Christians are enabled to commune and through whom they are brought to God. Also, from the New Testament onward, Christians characteristically sang hymns to God that celebrate God's acts and attributes as well as the work and significance of God's Son. In short, in the proclamation and the religious practice reflected in the New Testament and characteristic of 'mainstream' Christian traditions down through the centuries, the significance of Jesus' redemptive and revealing work is seen and celebrated as deriving from his status as the unique agent of God's will. That is, the meaning of Christ is always expressed in terms of his relationship to God. All of the claims made about Christ in the New Testament have to do with significance that derives from God.[13] Even in the notion of Christ as divine Son from all eternity, this definition of Christ in relation to God (the Father) remains clear.

---

[12] See, e.g., Jungmann, *The Place of Christ in Liturgical Prayer*.

[13] See, e.g., the helpful discussions by Kreitzer (*Jesus and God in Paul's Eschatology*) and especially the more broad-ranging analysis of Paul's language for God and Christ by Richardson (*Paul's Language about God*).

Christians are called to love and worship God with minds as well as hearts. Our Muslim and Jewish neighbours sometimes express anxiety about Christian monotheism, though that anxiety seems to Christians too often misinformed about traditional Christian teaching. Of course, despite the disapproval of adherents of other monotheistic traditions, Christians cannot easily forego or object to the worship of Jesus and continue to think they represent Christian tradition. But we Christians are bound, not merely by the demands of others but even more forcefully by our own professed monotheistic stance, to worship Christ within a commitment to the one God, recognising Jesus as the unique Son of God the Father. The concerns of Muslims and Jews can be heard appreciatively by Christians as reminders to us of our own profession to confess and worship one God.

As I have indicated already, this monotheistic concern is in fact what lies behind the central Christian doctrine of the Tri-une God. A strong commitment to maintaining a monotheistic stance necessitated the rather lengthy and complex theological debates and formulations of the early Christian centuries. Had these Christians not been anxious to be monotheists, their life would have been much simpler! It was not difficult to deify a new god or demi-god in the Roman world, and Christians could have done this with Jesus readily enough.[14] Indeed, the developed Christian gnostic systems show that some ancient Christians were not terribly concerned with monotheism and instead projected a radical multiplicity of divinities.[15] But the

---

[14] See, e.g., Lösch's study (*Deitas Jesu und Antike Apotheose: Ein Beitrag zur Exegese und Religionsgeschichte*), which gives attention to the deification of human rulers in the Roman world.

[15] Michael Williams has challenged the notion that there was a cohesive 'gnosticism', but it is clear that there were Christian groups whose beliefs reflect the lack of concern with monotheism to which I refer here. In fact, it is interesting to note how in a number of the relevant texts often identified as 'gnostic' the exclusivist claims of *Yahweh* such as Isaiah 45:21-22, which are central texts for Jewish and Christian monotheistic beliefs, are treated as the misinformed or lying statements of an inferior god (e.g., *The Apocryphon of John* 11.20 [Robinson (ed.), *The Nag Hammadi Library in English*, 111]).

dominant (or at least ultimately the more viable) Christian concern was to develop an understanding of Jesus' divine significance *within the framework of faith in one God*.[16] Christian thinkers ransacked the vocabulary and conceptual categories of the ancient world, and when those did not suffice they even invented new categories and new meanings for words in an effort to develop and articulate a faith and rationale for Christian devotional practice that both accorded Christ full reverence as divine yet also retained a monotheistic stance.[17]

If I may speak directly to fellow Christians, let us see that our practical worship as well as our profession is genuinely trinitarian, and that Christian truth and Christian worship accord with each other. It would be a healthy exercise for Christians to reflect on the meaning of the one God in our devotional life, and to develop prayer practice that does not willy-nilly confuse God and Jesus, but celebrates the unique divine Son as from the one God. Study of the prayer expressions in the New Testament and in the liturgies and prayers of Christian tradition (such as the *Book of Common Prayer*, which was shaped by centuries of Christian worship practice) would provide helpful stimulus and resources.

Worship of God and Christian Identity

The worship of Jesus within the context of biblical monotheism and Christian trinitarian teaching also has profound

---

[16] See, e.g., Lortz, 'Das Christentum als Monotheismus in den Apologien des zweiten Jahrhunderts' in Koeniger (ed.), *Beiträge zur Geschichte des christlichen Altertums und der Byzantinischen Literatur: Festgabe Albert Ehrhard*; Osborn, *The Emergence of Christian Theology*.

[17] An example of ancient Christian innovation in terminology and meanings can be seen in their appropriation of the Latin term *persona* and the development of a new and distinctively Christian meaning for the Greek term *hypostasis* in their efforts to articulate how belief in 'one God' could accommodate the threefold shape of early Christian religious experience and convictions. See, e.g., Wiles, *The Making of Christian Doctrine: A Study in the Principles of Early Doctrinal Development*, 130–40.

implications for Christian self-understanding and for Christian views about salvation. Christians traditionally worship Jesus as the *unique* Son of God the Father. This uniqueness of Jesus' sonship is important.

This unique sonship means that the relationship of Christians to God is to be understood as *derivative*, and is not properly seen as possessed by Christians by nature or as an inherent property, but as bestowed by God's grace *through Christ*.[18] For example, Paul portrays the filial relationship of believers to God as bestowed through Jesus, the paradigmatic Son of God. Jesus is the 'first-born among many brethren' (Rom. 8:29), and the Spirit of God's Son, Jesus, bestows on believers a sense of their filial relationship to God (Gal. 4:6).[19] We Christians traditionally worship Jesus as the divinely-appointed-for-us access to God. That is, we worship Jesus because of who he is and because of the divinely assigned role he plays in redemption as mediator and redeemer. Unless we understand the New Testament appraisal of the human predicament, which amounts to a moral and spiritual alienation from the one true God, we will not appreciate the significance of Jesus as God's unique Son sent to offer reconciliation and adoption into a filial relationship with God. Nor will we understand that this filial relationship derives from Jesus' unique sonship.

We Christians worship God *in Jesus' name and through Jesus*. I am not at all sure that the meaning of this is well enough understood among Christians. To pray in Jesus' name and through him means that we enter into Jesus' status in God's favour, and invoke Jesus' standing with God and the efficacy of his redeeming work (over against our own sinful deficits) to be given access to God. In this light, Christians do not properly

---

[18] For further discussion, see Torrance, *Community, and the Triune God of Grace*, esp. 6–31.

[19] On Paul's use of divine sonship language for Christ, see Hurtado, 'Son of God', in Hawthorne and Martin (eds.) *Dictionary of Paul and His Letters*. On the theme in Romans, see Hurtado, 'Jesus' Divine Sonship' in Paul's Epistle to the Romans' in Soderlund and Wright (eds.) *Romans and the People of God: Essays in Honor of Gordon D. Fee on the Occasion of His 65th Birthday*.

approach God as an expression of some ill-founded sentimentality about God's 'daddy-hood'. Christians properly call God 'Father' neither to make God 'sire' of the world or of us, nor because we want to deify fatherhood and maleness, but instead precisely because we enter into *Jesus'* relationship to God as Father. We are to consider ourselves as enfranchised into Jesus' sonship with God.

We affirm Jesus' intimacy with and revelation of God by echoing and affirming Jesus' own relation to God in our prayer forms. As we have noted earlier, in the New Testament, God is 'the God and Father *of our Lord Jesus Christ*' (e.g., Eph. 1:3; 2 Cor. 1:3; Rom. 15:6; 1 Pet. 1:3), and, thus, Christians should understand that we address God as 'our Father' derivatively and as an expression of our acknowledgement of Jesus' sonship. We do this because Jesus' sonship is taken as powerfully effective in redemption on our behalf, bringing Christians into Jesus' standing with God (e.g., Heb. 2:10–18).

The term 'Father' in the prayer traditionally known as the 'Our Father' (the so-called 'Lord's Prayer') is formally remembered in the canonical gospel accounts as *given* to Christian practice by Jesus (Matt. 6:7–14; Luke 11:1–4), where this prayer and this form of address to God are presented as taught to the disciples by Jesus. And Paul makes the invocation of God as 'Father' a manifestation of the Spirit of God's Son in Christian believers (Rom. 8:9–17, esp. vv. 15–16; Gal. 4:4–6).[20] Christian practice alludes to this recognition of our dependent and bestowed filial status in the traditional introductions to praying the 'Our Father', as when the liturgical leader prompts a Christian group to join in saying the prayer with the words, 'As our Saviour taught us . . .' or 'Wherefore,

---

[20] Unfortunately, a certain sentimentalising of the New Testament notion of God as Father has become attached to the New Testament term 'Abba'. Contrary to this sentimentalising notion, 'Abba' does not connote 'Daddy'. See esp. the studies by Barr ('Abba Isn't "Daddy" ', *Journal of Theological Studies* n.s. 39 [1988], 28–47) and D'Angelo ('Abba and "Father": Imperial Theology and the Jesus Traditions', *Journal of Biblical Literature* 111 [1992], 611–30).

we are bold to say . . .' (and in the 'wherefore' hangs the tale behind the boldness!).

Worship and Patriarchy

Some modern feminist criticism is both unfounded and yet also instructive for Christian worship. It is unfounded to claim that to reverence and address God as 'Father' and to reverence and refer to Jesus as 'the Son' *necessarily* means to privilege maleness and to give it transcendent validation while denying this to femaleness and motherhood. This sort of feminist critique presumes that all worship is the straight projection and divinisation of creaturely attributes such as maleness, and that the object of worship is some idealised version of the attributes of the worshipper. On this assumption, the demand is logically that both maleness and femaleness should be divinised. Otherwise, women have no such idealised object with which to identify themselves. Were these assumptions totally correct, the demand would appear to be compelling.

Properly informed, however, Christian worship of the Triune God is not (or at least is not supposed to involve) the deification of creaturely characteristics. Christian worship is not supposed to be the projection of our own attributes into ideal, divine status. This would be a deification of the creature, a self-worship, which is admittedly all too accurate as characterising human 'religiousness'. But from the standpoint of biblical tradition, any such *de facto* divinisation of the creature manifests a distance from the effectual revelation of the true and living God. Worship that is offered in response to the revealed, true and living God should seek to avoid any deification of the creature.

Both Old Testament and New Testament texts warn against worshipping any projection of ourselves. In biblical tradition, all deification of the creature, including the worship of any human attribute or faculty, constitutes idolatry. For example, Deuteronomy 4:15–20 forbids making any 'image' of God drawn from creaturely categories or phenomena and used as object of worship, and the passage significantly includes 'male or female' (v. 16) among the creaturely characteristics that must not be worshipped. Among well-known New Testament passages, Romans 1:18–23 captures the essential nature of idolatry as consisting precisely in the confusion of the creature with the Creator. In this passage as well, the confusion condemned includes images 'resembling a mortal human being' (*en homoiomati eikonos phthartou anthropou, v. 23*).

For this reason, we can object that it is a red herring to associate automatically the worship of the God and Father of the Lord Jesus Christ, worship offered through this unique Son, with the deification of the 'male'. Clear biblical and theological teachings show that, properly understood and properly practised, Christian worship should not be liable to such criticism. Christians are to reverence God as 'Father' only because we enter into Jesus' own filial relationship to God, not because of a desire to glorify maleness or paternity over femaleness and motherhood.

But, sadly, a great deal of Christian worship is in fact not properly informed by the Bible and Christian theological and liturgical tradition, including the worship of some who may think of themselves as very traditional and orthodox! In light of this, the feminist criticism of Christian worship is valid and instructive in pointing to a version of idolatry that might otherwise go undetected, simply because it may have become so familiar, may seem so 'natural' and may be expressed in terms drawn from Christian tradition. Worshipping God 'in Spirit and in truth', however, means seeking to rise above any such idolatrous privileging of this or that place, this or that language, this or that ethnicity, and any other aspect of creaturehood.[21]

---

[21] I allude here, of course, to John 4:20–24, which is particularly fertile for the topic of what true worship should be in light of gender questions. Space prevents anything more than some brief pointers for further reflection on the possible significance of this passage. (1) The dialogue in John 4:7–26 is clearly quite deliberately one of Jesus and a woman, and readers frequently note the undertone of sexual tension in the dialogue (e.g., v. 9, 'Do you ask me, being a

Perhaps one important way for Christians and others to tell if particular Christian worship really is 'in Spirit and truth' in this sense is to discern whether reference to God as 'Father' is matched in our lives by a privileging of maleness, a feudal-like hierarchy of one creaturely characteristic over others. If our lives show a preferential treatment of maleness, for example, it may well be that our Christian worship has been allowed to devolve into an idolatry that is no less damnable in spite of its use of Christian terminology (indeed, Christian distortion of the revelation of God should be seen by Christians as doubly reprehensible). Particularly, if reference to God as 'Father' is taken as *justifying* the privileging of the male gender, then this certainly shows a serious failure to understand the Christian theological rationale and meaning of the term 'Father' as a form of address to God. In this situation, the feminist critique of 'Father' rings true and is a judgement to be received gratefully.

The heavenly 'Father' should be worshipped, not as an extension of ourselves, as justifying partriarchy, but worshipped truly as the one God who is categorically transcendent over the creature. That is, as 'Father' only through Jesus Christ. This God transcends creation and thereby reveals and judges its inadequacy in representing God, as well as our abuse of our creaturely features such as gender. But at the same time this transcendent God, precisely by being transcendent beyond creaturely attributes, is able to affirm, validate and

---

[21] *(continued)* woman of Samaria?'). (2) In her conversation here and in her life as well the woman identifies herself entirely in terms of males (her references to 'our father Jacob', v. 12, and 'our fathers', v. 20; her multiple relationships with men in vv. 16–18). In this light, the promise of a new worship of 'the Father' based on 'the Spirit and truth' (the first term probably identifying the latter, i.e., 'the Spirit who is truth') may be taken here as including a transcending of the privileging of human traditions which are characterised by their male dominance. This is likely reflected in the Evangelist's depiction of Jesus' revelation to the woman and in her becoming the trustworthy witness to other Samaritans (v. 39). It is increasingly clear to scholars that the various narratives of the Gospel of John reflect (and were intended to speak to) the concerns and the experiences of the early Christians for whom it was written.

redeem the whole of the creation (Rom. 8:18–23), including our maleness and femaleness (Gal. 2:28–29). Given the gender-inclusive shape of God's redemption, it is important as Christians to ask ourselves whether this equal validation of male and female is evident in our lives, our families and our wider relationships, whether the inherent value of the creation (inherent to creation as God's beloved creature) and the equal importance and worth of male and female are demonstrated in our church life? Theology can play a role in helping to guide us to right living (though, to be sure, the right living to which Christians are summoned requires a real transformation and not merely instruction). But it is also true that the character of our particular Christian living is in turn a good indication of how we really understand and mean what we profess to be our theological beliefs. That is, our living is a very good reflection of how 'good' our theology really is!

Of course, all theology reflects sociological factors. This is why I advocate testing the meaning of our theological language by examining our social practices. Social circumstances and conditions can also contribute to theological reflection and even to reformation. For example, revulsion at the Nazi policy of Jewish extermination has helped to produce in the post-World War II years a greater Christian awareness of anti-Semitism in Christian theology and traditions.[22] But careful, incisive theological reflection can also promote reformed social realities. Perhaps Christian reflection on the proper meaning of God as 'Father' (and on the idolatrous uses of the term to which Christians are prone) could contribute to overcoming the patriarchy that Christians inherited from their various cultures and that has been so uncritically appropriated and validated in Christian practice.

Feminist critique of Christian practice is fair comment in so far as it highlights an uncritical Christian appropriation of what is now termed 'patriarchy'. This patriarchy denies proper validity and dignity to the female, and this is a sin, as well as being objectionable to those with feminist concerns. It is both an offence against women and also a sin of idolatry

---

[22] See, e.g., Klein, *Anti-Judaism in Christian Theology*.

against God. In other words, there are not only humanitarian reasons for identifying patriarchy. There are also profoundly theological reasons that have to do with distinguishing the revelation of God from heretical and distorting images.

Worship Earthly and Transcendent

I turn now to another important matter. As we noted in our discussion of early Christian worship conceptions and practice, from the New Testament onward there is the notion that worship should be understood as an earthly participation in a heavenly reality. In chapter two, I noted that this sense of participation in heavenly worship lies behind the traditional phrasing 'Wherefore, with angels, archangels and all the company of heaven we laud and magnify your glorious name', wording which introduces the congregational recitation or chanting of the 'Trisagion' (Greek for 'thrice holy', taken from the song of the heavenly creatures in Isaiah 6:3) in the liturgical traditions of Christian Eucharist.[23] The introductory phrasing and the Trisagion together express the idea that the earthly praise of the Christian congregation is to be offered in imitation of, and in concert with, the true praise of God by 'all the company of heaven'. As we noted in chapter two, the New Testament bears witness that from the beginning believers saw their humble worship gatherings in small groups in houses as events with this transcendent significance and character.

In our time, it will be a challenge for Christians to re-appropriate meaningfully the idea of being in the presence of angels in worship, and the meaning of the notion that earthly worship can be a participation in the liturgy of heaven itself.[24] Traditional hymns such as 'Ye watchers and ye holy ones', or 'Crown him with many crowns', and hymnic appeals such as

---

[23] See Cross and Livingstone, *Oxford Dictionary of the Christian Church*, 1395–6.

[24] On the transcendent and modernity, see Berger, *A Rumour of Angels: Modern Society and the Rediscovery of the Supernatural*.

'angels help us to adore him' will all pass right by modern Christians or strike us as merely quaint unless we seek to encounter again and appropriate in ways meaningful for moderns the significance behind these images and traditions.

We modern, westernised Christians could well do with lifting our liturgical eyes beyond the alternatives of either shallow notions of 'relevance' or the frozen formality against which demands for 'relevance' are often raised, and beyond the alternatives of either merely human elegance or austere plainness, to an approach to worship that makes us conscious of its 'vertical' reality and significance. This is not a matter of guitars versus organs, sedate style versus 'happy-clappy'. If Christian worship has transcendent significance, it is not by virtue of particular liturgical styles or practices but by our worship really being the worship of the one God and of the one who, having been made Christ and Lord, sits at God's 'right hand', bearing unique divine favour and authority. That is, if Christian worship is genuinely offered to the one true transcendent God to whose revelation it claims to respond, then this transcendent God alone gives to earthly worship any hope of significance higher than merely earthly conventions and transactions. But Christians can perhaps experience and participate more consciously, deliberately and fully in that transcendent reality if we learn from the New Testament and Christian tradition and seek to inform and inspire modern Christian attitudes toward worship with its higher possibilities.

Meeting for worship with a sense of being in the presence of God, gathered before God, the participants aligning themselves with heavenly realities, is not the same thing as a club or business meeting or a folksy effort at merely developing familiarity with one another. Of course, Christians will want to develop strong relationships and build the networks of acquaintance that we humans need. But Christians will also need to recognise that all our efforts are supported and contextualised by the divine reality and purposes that we invoke and that call us together as an *ekklesia*, a group meeting with 'official' significance and a high calling as God's people.

Worship and Eschatology

Another feature of earliest Christian worship that bears reflection for possible meaning today is its strong eschatological flavour. In terms of New Testament precedent, Christian worship should be understood as an anticipation and declaration of the final triumph of God and God's purposes in Christ. In theological terms, Christian acclamation of Jesus as *Kyrios* (Lord) is, thus, an eschatological action, orienting participants toward the ultimate outcome of God's redemptive purposes. The motif of the presence of angels in the worship gathering mentioned earlier in this discussion alerts Christians to a higher loyalty and citizenship and the deeper dimensions of reality. Just so, a recognition that acclamation by the earthly historical congregation derives from God's exaltation of Jesus and also anticipates the future universal acclamation of Jesus as Lord can lift the eyes of the worshipping congregation beyond the routines and mundane acts of liturgy, beyond mere religious honorifics. An awareness that Christian worship has this eschatological dimension can set faces of participants toward the coming dawn of Christ's redemptive victory and the summing up of all things in Christ that is asserted in Christian proclamation.

From Constantine onward, imperial Christianity lost the earlier understanding of itself as the provisional witness to the Kingdom of God, and quickly imagined itself to be that Kingdom in its own structures and earthly prominence (which had in fact been established under Constantine by very familiar use of imperial force). Likewise, imperial Christianity lost the earlier keenness of eschatological hope, and settled down into what became a more humdrum routine of religious acts for their own sake. But essential to the proclamation embodied in the New Testament is the understanding that all our actions stand against the horizon of God's ultimate triumph in grace through Jesus Christ. Only with a view toward, and a hope for, God's eschatological victory over all that diminishes and destroys creation can Christian action have any meaning greater than merely one curious version of human endeavour.

More specifically, Christian worship could be re-enlivened and enriched by remembering the larger picture of God's purposes, which extend beyond our own immediate setting and time to take in all human history and which promise a future victory over evil and a consummation of redeeming grace. Apart from a hope in God's triumph over evil, apart from a confidence that Jesus really is the divinely appointed Lord in whom all things are to find their meaning, Christian acclamation of Jesus as Lord is a stupid thing, refuted and mocked by the powerful, negative realities of our creaturehood: the political and economic tyrannies, religious and irreligious forces, and social and cultural developments that make Christian faith seem trivial and our worship little more than a quaint avocation.

Christ-Devotion and Political Claims

This also has to be said, perhaps even more so in the light of twentieth-century experience of totalitarian political regimes. Properly understood, worship of God, and of Jesus as the unique divine Son of the one God, also involves the withholding of worship and unqualified obedience from any other who may claim it. In the New Testament the characteristic affirmation that distinguished Christian worship was: 'Jesus is Lord'. In the first few centuries, Christians recognised that this acclamation meant tensions with the divine claims and absolute demands of the Roman system, and in subsequent times Christians have frequently been given occasions to face a similarly stark choice.[25] Like our Jewish cousins, Christians classically pray(ed) *for* the earthly ruler, not *to* the ruler. Christian monotheistic faith prevents anything else, if we are true to it. Any

---

[25] Note the collection of primary texts in Guyot and Klein (*Das frühe Christentum bis zum Ende der Verfolgungen*, Band 1: *Die Christen im heidnischen Staat*. Texte zur Forschung 60). The scholarly literature on Christian conflict with the Roman state is vast. Among recent studies, see Keresztes (*Imperial Rome and the Christians: From Herod the Great to about 200 A.D.*).

Christian political loyalty must stop well short of giving the ruler or regime total and uncritical submission.

Earliest Christian reverence of Christ often involved a deliberate use of terms and titles that were also claimed by the Roman system, such as 'Son of God'.[26] Thus, early Christian reverence of Christ was at the same time a religious act and also one with profound political connotations and consequences. In confessing Jesus as '*the* Lord' and '*the* Son of God', these early Christians unavoidably, and often quite knowingly, denied this sort of status to the Roman ruler.[27]

Our temporal and geographical placement in modern, secular democracies may not present us with the same obvious competition between worshipping Christ and undue reverence of rulers or other objects. We are not required to offer incense to the ruler's image or to join in the worship of civic gods. But perhaps part of the reason for the modern Western difficulty in seeing how early Christian worship is instructive for our understanding of our relationship to other claimants for our loyalty is that our perception of what we are supposed to be doing in our worship of Christ is so poor! I suggest that a dedicated and collective commitment to meaningful, thoughtful and genuine worship of 'Him who sits on the throne and the Lamb' (Rev. 5:13) would sharpen our vision for seeing the inappropriate (even if familiar) demands made upon us in our cultures, and help us to see whether in our own ways today we Christians may be countenancing 'things sacrificed to idols' (Rev. 2:14, 20). Our idolatrous tendencies may seem to us more subtle, but may be no less of a contradiction to Christian professions of faith. A more profound understanding of Christian faith would equip contemporary Christians better in our social and political lives as well as in the more familiar areas of

---

[26] Still valuable for its citation of primary evidence is Deissmann's discussion of early Christian usage of rhetoric also used in Roman imperial propaganda and cultus, *Light from the Ancient East*, 338–78.

[27] The characteristic use of the definite article in New Testament acclamations of Jesus with these titles carries an implicitly exclusive connotation.

private morality to which some forms of Christian piety devote almost exclusive attention.

Conclusion

In this final chapter, I have proposed that the worship of Christians today should be informed and enriched by biblical teachings and that worship should be conducted thoughtfully in the light of the need to distinguish between mere human religion (which is always idolatrous in tendency, whether Christian or non-Christian) and the revelation of God. Precisely if worship seems a familiar activity to contemporary Christians, there is all the more reason to do some serious reflection, taking nothing for granted and considering afresh the meanings and implications of Christian devotion.

Christian worship of the one God is offered through Jesus, and also jointly to him with God. As we have seen, worship of Jesus is not merely worship of an additional god, or some reverence of a divine hero after the pattern of the Roman religious environment of earliest Christianity. Nor does it represent the supplanting of an old, obsolete deity by a younger one. Worship of Jesus properly is worship of the one God, through, and revealed in a unique way in, Jesus Christ. Thus, intelligent worship of Jesus involves bringing to that worship a grasp of what the gospel of Jesus Christ tells us of God's purposes. Reflecting today on the worship of Jesus can lead Christians to a deeper discovery of God and of who Christians are called to be in God's redemptive grace.

Bibliography

Albright, W. F., 'A Biblical Fragment from the Maccabean Age: The Nash Papyrus', *Journal of Biblical Literature* 56 (1937), 145–76.

Anderson, G. A., 'Sacrifice and Sacrificial Offerings (OT)' in Freedman, D. N. (ed.) *Anchor Bible Dictionary*. 6 vols. (Garden City: Doubleday, 1992), 5: 871–86.

Armstrong, A. H. (ed.), *Classical Mediterranean Spirituality: Egyptian, Greek, Roman* (New York: Crossroad, 1986).

Aune, David E., *The Cultic Setting of Realized Eschatology in Early Christianity*, Novum Testamentum Supplements 28 (Leiden: Brill, 1972).

——, *Prophecy in Early Christianity and the Ancient Mediterranean World* (Grand Rapids: Eerdmans, 1983).

——, 'Worship, Early Christian' in Freedman, D. N. (ed.) *Anchor Bible Dictionary*. 6 vols. (Garden City: Doubleday, 1992), 6: 973–89.

——, 'Magic in Early Christianity' in H. Temporini and W. Haase (eds.) *Aufstieg und Niedergang der römischen Welt* (Berlin: De Gruyter), 2.23/2: 1507–57.

Banks, Robert, *Paul's Idea of Community: The Early House Churches in their Historical Setting* (Grand Rapids: Eerdmans, 1980).

Barr, James, 'Abba Isn't "Daddy" ', *Journal of Theological Studies* n.s. 39 (1988), 28–47.

Barton, John, 'Prophecy (Postexilic Hebrew)' in Freedman, D. N. (ed.) *Anchor Bible Dictionary*. 6 vols. (Garden City: Doubleday, 1992), 5:489–95.

Bauckham, Richard J., 'The Worship of Jesus in Apocalyptic Christianity', *New Testament Studies* 27 (1981), 322–41 (revised and expanded version in R. J. Bauckham, *The Climax of the Covenant: Studies on the Book of Revelation*, [Edinburgh: T. & T. Clark, 1993], 118–49).

——, Jesus, Worship of' in Freedman, D. N. (ed.) *Anchor Bible Dictionary*. 6 vols. (Garden City: Doubleday, 1992), 3:812–19.

——, *God Crucified: Monotheism and Christology in the New Testament* (Carlisle: Paternoster, 1998).

Bauer, Walter; Arndt, William F.; Gingrich, Wilbur F. and Danker, Frederick W., *A Greek-English Lexicon of the New Testament and Other Early Christian Literature* (Chicago: University of Chicago Press, 1979²).

Beasley-Murray, G. R., *Baptism in the New Testament* (Grand Rapids: Eerdmans, 1962).

Beck, Roger, 'Mithraism since Franz Cumont' in H. Temporini and W. Haase (eds.) *Aufstieg und Niedergang der römischen Welt* (Berlin: De Gruyter), 2.17: 2003–2115.

Benko, Stephen, *Pagan Rome and the Early Christians* (London: Batsford, 1985).

Berger, Peter L., *A Rumour of Angels: Modern Society and the Rediscovery of the Supernatural* (London: Allen Lane, 1970).

Beyreuther, E. and Finkenrath, G., 'Joy, Rejoice' in Colin Brown (ed.), *The New International Dictionary of New Testament Theology*. 3 vols. (Grand Rapids: Zondervan, 1975–78), 2:352–61.

Bevan, Edwyn, *Holy Images: An Inquiry into Idolatry and Image-Worship in Ancient Paganism and in Christianity* (London: George Allen & Unwin, 1940).

Bickerman, Elias, 'Symbolism in the Dura Synagogue' in Bickerman, *Studies in Jewish and Christian History*, Part Three (Leiden: Brill, 1986), pp. 225–44.

Black, Matthew, 'The Maranatha Invocation and Jude 14, 15 (1 Enoch 1:9)' in B. Lindars and S. S. Smalley (eds.), *Christ and Spirit in the New Testament* (Cambridge: Cambridge University Press, 1973), pp. 189–96.

Blue, Bradley, 'Acts and the House Church' in David W. J. Gill, Conrad Gempf (eds.) *The Book of Acts in its Graeco-Roman Setting* (Carlisle: Paternoster; Grand Rapids: Eerdmans, 1994), pp. 119–222.

Bokser, Baruch M., 'Unleavened Bread and Passover, Feasts of' in Freedman, D. N. (ed.) *Anchor Bible Dictionary*. 6 vols. (Garden City: Doubleday, 1992), 6:755–65.

Boring, M. E., 'Prophecy (Early Christian)' in Freedman, D. N. (ed.) *Anchor Bible Dictionary*. 6 vols. (Garden City: Doubleday, 1992), 5:495–502.

Borgen, Peder, ' "Yes," "No," "How Far?"': The Participation of Jews and Christians in Pagan Cults' in Troels Engberg-Pedersen (ed.), *Paul in His Hellenistic Context* (Minneapolis: Fortress Press, 1995), pp. 30–59.

Bradshaw, Paul, *The Search for the Origins of Christian Worship* (London: SPCK, 1992).

Brooks, J. A., 'Kiss of Peace' in E. Ferguson (ed.), *Encyclopedia of Early Christianity* (New York/(London: Garland Publishing, 1990), pp. 521–22.

Cabaniss, Alan, *Pattern in Early Christian Worship* (Macon, Ga.: Mercer University Press, 1989).

Casanova, José, *Public Religions in the Modern World* (Chicago/London: University of Chicago Press, 1994).

Casey, Maurice, *From Jewish Prophet to Gentile God* (Cambridge: James Clarke; Louisville: Westminster/John Knox Press, 1991).

Charlesworth, J. H., 'Jewish Hymns, Odes, and Prayers (ca. 167 B.C.E.–135 C.E.)' in R. A. Kraft and G. W. E. Nickelsburg (eds.), *Early Judaism and its Modern Interpreters* (Atlanta: Scholars Press, 1986), pp. 411–36.

——, (ed.). *The Old Testament Pseudepigrapha*. 2 vols. (Garden City: Doubleday, 1983–85).

Coenen, L., 'Church', *The New International Dictionary of New Testament Theology*, ed. Colin Brown. 3 vols. (Grand Rapids: Zondervan, 1975–78), 1:291–307.

Conzelmann, Hans, 'Christus im Gottesdienst der neutestamentlichen Zeit' in H. Conzelmann, *Theologie als Schriftauslegung: Aufsätze zum Neuen Testament* (Munich: Christian Kaiser, 1974), pp. 120–30.

——, *1 Corinthians*. Hermeneia Commentaries (Philadelphia: Fortress, 1975).

Cragg, Kenneth, *The Christ and the Faiths* (London: SPCK; Philadelphia: Westminster Press, 1986).

Cross, F. L. and Livingstone, E. A., *Oxford Dictionary of the Christian Church* (Oxford: Oxford University Press, 1983²).

Cullmann, Oscar, *Baptism in the New Testament*. Studies in Biblical Theology 1 (London: SCM, 1950).

——, *Early Christian Worship*. Studies in Biblical Theology 10 (London: SCM, 1953).

——, 'The Meaning of the Lord's Supper in Primitive Christianity' in O. Cullmann and F. J. Leenhardt, *Essays on the Lord's Supper* (Richmond: John Knox Press, 1958), pp. 5–23.

——, *Prayer in the New Testament* (Minneapolis: Fortress, 1994).

D'Angelo, M. R., 'Abba and "Father"; Imperial Theology and the Jesus Traditions', *Journal of Biblical Literature* 111 (1992), 611–30.

Davidson, Maxwell J., *Angels at Qumran: A Comparative Study of 1 Enoch 1–36, 72–108 and Sectarian Writings from Qumran*. Journal for the Study of the Pseudepigrapha Supplements 11 (Sheffield: JSOT Press, 1992).

Davis, C. J., *The Name and Way of the Lord: Old Testament Themes, New Testament Christology*. Journal for the Study of the New Testament Supplements 129 (Sheffield: Sheffield Academic Press, 1996).

Deichgräber, Reinhard, *Gotteshymnus und Christushymnus in der frühen Christenheit*. Studien zur Umwelt des Neuen Testament 5 (Göttingen: Vandenhoeck & Ruprecht, 1967).

Deissmann, Adolf, *Light from the Ancient East*, trans. L. R. M. Strachan (Grand Rapids: Baker Book House, 1965; original publication, 1927).

——, *Bible Studies*, trans. A. Grieve (Edinburgh: T. & T. Clark, 1901).

——, 'The Name "Jesus" ' in G. K. A. Bell and D. A. Deissmann (eds.) *Mysterium Christi: Christological Studies by British and German Theologians* (London: Longmans, Greek & Co., 1930), pp. 3–27.

Delling, Gerhard, *Worship in the New Testament* (London: Darton, Longman & Todd, 1962).

Dölger, F. J., *Sol Salutis: Gebet und Gesang im christlichen Altertum mit besonderer Rücksicht auf die Ostung in Gebet und Liturgie* (Münster: Aschenforffsche Verlagsbuchhandlung, 1972^2 [1925]).

Dunn, J. D. G., *Jesus and the Spirit* (London: SCM; Philadelphia: Westminster Press, 1975).

———, *The Theology of Paul the Apostle* (Edinburgh: T. & T. Clark; Grand Rapids: Eerdmans, 1998).

Egan, R. B., 'Isis: Goddess of the *Oikoumene*' in L. W. Hurtado (ed.) *Goddesses in Religions and Modern Debate*. University of Manitoba Studies in Religion 1 (Atlanta: Scholars Press, 1990), pp. 123–42.

Elbogen, I., *Der jüdische Gottesdienst in seiner geschichtlichen Entwicklung* (Frankfurt am Main: J. Kauffmann Verlag, 1931; reprint Hildesheim: Georg Olms Verlag, 1995).

Enermalm-Ogawa, Agneta, *Un langage de prière juif en grec: Le temoinage des deux premieres livres des Maccabées* (Uppsala: Almquist & Wiksell, 1987).

Falk, Daniel K., 'Jewish Prayer Literature and the Jerusalem Church in Acts' in Richard Bauckham (ed.), *The Book of Acts in its First Century Setting. Vol. 4: The Book of Acts in its Palestinian Setting* (Carlisle: Paternoster; Grand Rapids: Eerdmans, 1995), pp. 267–301.

Fee, Gordon D., *The First Epistle to the Corinthians*. New International Commentary on the New Testament (Grand Rapids: Eerdmans, 1987).

———, *God's Empowering Presence: The Holy Spirit in the Letters of Paul* (Peabody, Mass.: Hendrickson, 1994).

Ferguson, Everett, *Backgrounds of Early Christianity* (Grand Rapids: Eerdmans, 1987).

Finegan, Jack, *Myth & Mystery: An Introduction to the Pagan Religions of the Biblical World* (Grand Rapids: Baker, 1989).

Finney, P. C., *The Invisible God: The Earliest Christians on Art* (Oxford: Oxford University Press, 1994).

Fitzmyer, J. A., 'A Feature of Qumran Angelology and the Angels of 1 Cor 11:10', *New Testament Studies* 4 (1957–58), 48–58; reprinted in J. A. Fitzmyer, *Essays on the Semitic Background of the New Testament* (Missoula: Scholars Press, 1974), pp. 187–204; and in J. A. Fitzmyer, *The Semitic Background of the New Testament* (Grand Rapids: Eerdmans, 1997), pp. 187–204.

Fletcher-Louis, Crispin H. T., *Luke–Acts: Angels, Christology and Soteriology*. Wissenschaftliche Untersuchungen zum Neuen Testament 2/94 (Tübingen: J. C. B. Mohr [Paul Siebeck], 1997).

Flusser, David, 'Psalms, Hymns and Prayers' in M. E. Stone (ed.), *Jewish Writings of the Second Temple Period*. CRINT 2/2 (Assen: Van Gorcum; Philadelphia: Fortress Press, 1984), pp. 551–77.

Foerster, Werner, 'κυριακός' in G. Kittel and G. Friedrich (eds.), *Theological Dictionary of the New Testament*, trans. G. Bromiley. 10 vols. (Grand Rapids: Eerdmans, 1964–76), 3:1095–96.

Galling. K. (ed.) *Die Religion in Geschichte und Gegenwart*. 7 vols. (Tübingen: J. C. B. Mohr, 1957–65³). Gärtner, Bertil, *The Temple and Community in Qumran and the New Testament*. Society for New Testament Studies Monograph Series 1 (Cambridge: Cambridge University Press, 1965).

Gill, David W. J. and Winter, Bruce W., 'Acts and Roman Religion' in David W. J. Gill and Conrad Gempf (eds.) *The Book of Acts in its Graeco-Roman Setting* (Carlisle: Paternoster; Grand Rapids: Eerdmans, 1994), pp. 79–103.

Gillespie, Thomas W., *The First Theologians: A Study in Early Christian Prophecy* (Grand Rapids: Eerdmans, 1994).

Grant, Robert M., *Gods and the One God* (Philadelphia: Westminster Press, 1986).

Graves, Robert (trans.), *The Transformations of Lucius otherwise known as the Golden Ass by Lucius Apuleius* (Harmondsworth: Penguin Books, 1950).

Greeven, H., 'προσκυνέω, προσκυνητής'. in G. Kittel and G. Friedrich (eds.), *Theological Dictionary of the New Testament*, trans. G. Bromiley. 10 vols. (Grand Rapids: Eerdmans, 1964–76), 6:758–66.

Griffiths, J. Guyn, 'Egypt and the Rise of the Synagogue' in Dan Urman and Paul V. M. Flesher (eds.), *Ancient Synagogues: Historical Analysis and Archaeological Discovery*. 2 vols. (Leiden: Brill, 1995), 1:3–16.

Grözinger, K. E., *Musik und Gesang in der Theologie der frühen jüdischen Literatur* (Tübingen: J. C. B. Mohr [Paul Siebeck], 1982).

Guthrie, W. K. C., 'Hymns' in N. G. L. Hammond and H. H. Scullard (eds.) *The Oxford Classical Dictionary* (Oxford: Clarendon, 1970²), p. 534.

Guyot, Peter and Klein, Richard, *Das frühe Christentum bis zum Ende der Verfolgungen*, Band 1: *Die Christen im heidnischen Staat*. Texte zur Forschung 60 (Darmstadt: Wissenschaftliche Buchgesellschaft, 1993).

Hachlili, Rachel, *Ancient Jewish Art and Archaeology in the Land of Israel*. Handbuch der Orientalistik 7 (Leiden: Brill, 1988).

——, 'Early Jewish Art and Architecture' in Freedman, D. N. (ed.) *Anchor Bible Dictionary*. 6 vols. (Garden City: Doubleday, 1992), 1:447–54.

Hahn, Ferdinand, *The Worship of the Early Church*, trans. D. E. Green (Philadelphia: Fortress, 1973).

Hamman, Adalbert, *La prière I. Le Nouveau Testament* (Tournai: Desclée, 1959).

——, 'La prière chrétienne et la prière païnne, formes et différences' in H. Temporini and W. Haase (eds.) *Aufstieg und Niedergang der römischen Welt* (Berlin: De Gruyter), 2.23/2: 1190–1247.

Hammond, N. G. L. and Scullard, H. H. (eds.), *The Oxford Classical Dictionary* (Oxford: Clarendon Press, 1970²).

Hartman, Lars, 'Baptism "into the name of Jesus" and Early Christology: Some Tentative Considerations', *Studia Theologica* 28 (1974), 21–48.

——, ' "Into the Name of Jesus" ', *New Testament Studies* 20 (1974), 432–40.

——, 'Baptism' in Freedman, D. N. (ed.) *Anchor Bible Dictionary*. 6 vols. (Garden City: Doubleday, 1992), 1:583–94.

——, *'Into the Name of the Lord Jesus': Baptism in the Early Church* (Edinburgh: T. & T. Clark, 1997.

——, 'Early Baptism-Early Christology' in A. J. Malherbe and W. A. Meeks (eds.) *The Future of Christology: Essays in Honor of Leander E. Keck* (Minneapolis: Fortress, 1993), pp. 191–201.

Hay, David M., *Glory at the Right Hand: Psalm 110 in Early Christianity*. Society of Biblical Literature Monograph Series 18 (Nashville: Abingdon, 1973).

Hayward, C. T. R., *The Jewish Temple: A Non-Biblical Sourcebook* (London: Routledge, 1996).

Hegedus, Tim, 'The Urban Expansion of the Isis Cult: A Quantitative Approach', *Studies in Religion/Sciences Religieuses* 27 (1998), 161–78.

Heitmüller, Wilhelm, *'Im Name Jesu': Eine sprach-und-religionsgeschichtlich Untersuchung zum Neuen Testament, speziell zur altchristlichen Taufe* (Göttingen: Vandenhoeck & Ruprecht, 1903).

Hengel, Martin, 'Hymns and Christology' in M. Hengel, *Between Jesus and Paul* (London: SCM, 1983), pp. 78–96.

——, 'The Song about Christ in Earliest Worship' in M. Hengel, *Studies in Early Christology* (Edinburgh: T. & T. Clark, 1995), pp. 227–91.

Herz, Peter, 'Bibliographie zum römischen Kaiserkult' in H. Temporini and W. Haase (eds.) *Aufstieg und Niedergang der römischen Welt* (Berlin: De Gruyter), 2.16/2: 833–910.

Hill, David, *New Testament Prophecy* (Atlanta: John Knox, 1979).

Hooker, M. D., 'Authority on Her Head: An Examination of 1 Cor 11:10', *New Testament Studies* 10 (1964), 410–16

Hopkins, Clark, *The Discovery of Dura Europos* (New Haven: Yale University Press, 1979).

Horbury, William, *Jewish Messianism and the Cult of Christ* (London: SCM, 1998).

——, 'The Cult of Christ and the Cult of the Saints', *New Testament Studies* 44 (1998), 444–69.

Horsley, G. H. R., 'Invitations to the *kline* of Sarapis' in Horsley (ed.), *New Documents Illustrating Early Christianity*, vol. 1 (North Ryde, NSW: Ancient History Documentary Centre, Macquarie University, 1981), pp. 5–9.

Horst, Johannes, *Proskynein: Zur Anbetung im Urchristentum nach ihrer religionsgeschichtlichen Eigenart.* Neutestamentliche Forschungen 3/2 (Gütersloh: Bertelsmann, 1932).

Hunter, A. M., *Paul and His Predecessors* (Philadelphia: Westminster, 1961).

Hurtado, L. W., *One God, One Lord: Early Christian Devotion and Ancient Jewish Monotheism* (Philadelphia: Fortress Press, 1988; Edinburgh: T. & T. Clark, 1998²).

——, 'Lord' in G. F. Hawthorne and R. P. Martin (eds.) *Dictionary of Paul and His Letters* (Downers Grove, Ill./Leicester, UK: InterVarsity Press, 1993), pp. 560–69.

——, 'Son of God' in G. F. Hawthorne and R. P. Martin (eds.) *Dictionary of Paul and His Letters* (Downers Grove, Ill./Leicester, UK: InterVarsity Press, 1993), pp. 900–6.

——, 'First-Century Jewish Monotheism', *Journal for the Study of the New Testament* 71 (1998), pp. 3–26.

——, 'The Origins of the Worship of Christ', *Themelios* 19/2 (January 1994), 4–8.

——, 'Christ-Devotion in the First Two Centuries: Reflections and a Proposal', *Toronto Journal of Theology* 12 (1996), 17–33.

——, 'Pre-70 CE Jewish Opposition to Christ-Devotion', *Journal of Theological Studies* n.s. 50 (1999), 35–58.

——, 'New Testament Studies at the Turn of the Millennium: Questions for the Discipline', *Scottish Journal of Theology*, forthcoming 1999.

——, 'Jesus' Divine Sonship in Paul's Epistle to the Romans' in Sven K. Soderlund and N. T. Wright (eds.) *Romans and the People of God: Essays in Honor of Gordon D. Fee on the Occasion of His 65th Birthday* (Grand Rapids: Eerdmans, 1999), pp. 217–33.

——, 'Religious Experience and Religious Innovation in the New Testament', *Journal of Religion*, forthcoming 2000.

Jaubert, Annie, *La notion d'alliance dans le judaïsme aux abords d l'ère chrétienne*. Studia Sorbonensia 6 (Paris: Éditions du Seuil, 1963).

Jeremias, Joachim, *Jerusalem in the Time of Jesus* (London: SCM, 1969).

Johnson, Luke T., *Religious Experience in Earliest Christianity* (Minneapolis: Fortress Press, 1998).

Johnson, N. B., *Prayer in the Apocrypha and Pseudepigrapha*. Society of Biblical Literature Monograph Series 2 (Philadelphia: Society of Biblical Literature, 1948).

Judge, E. A., 'The Early Christians as a Scholastic Community', *Journal of Religious History* 1 (1960/61), 4–15, 125–37.

Juel, Donald, *Messianic Exegesis: Christological Interpretation of the Old Testament in Early Christianity* (Philadelphia: Fortress, 1988).

Jungmann, Joseph, *The Place of Christ in Liturgical Prayer* trans. A. Peeler, revised edition (London/Dublin: Geoffrey Chapman, 1965²).

Kasher, Aryeh, 'Synagogues as "Houses of Prayer" and "Holy Places" in the Jewish Communities of Hellenistic and Roman Egypt' in Dan Urman and Paul V. M. Flesher (eds.), *Ancient Synagogues: Historical Analysis and Archaeological Discovery*. 2 vols. (Leiden: Brill, 1995), 1:205–20.

Kennel, Gunter, *Frühchristliche Hymnen? Gattungskritische Studien zur Frage nach den Leidern der frühen Christenheit.* Wissenschaftliche Monographien zur Alten und Neuen Testament 71 (Neukirchen-Vluyn: Neukirchener Verlag, 1995).

Kepel, Gilles, *The Revenge of God: The Resurgence of Islam, Christianity and Judaism in the Modern World* trans. Alan Braley (Cambridge: Polity Press, 1994; French original, Éditions du Seuil, 1991).

Keresztes, Paul, *Imperial Rome and the Christians: From Herod the Great to about 200 A.D.* 2 vols. (Lanham, Md.: University Press of America, 1989).

Kimelman, Reuven, 'The Shema and the Amidah: Rabbinic Prayer' in Mark Kiley (ed.), *Prayer from Alexander to Constantine: A Critical Anthology* (London/New York: Routledge, 1997), pp. 108–20.

Klauck, Hans-Josef, *Die religiöse Umwelt des Urchristentums*. 2 vols. (Stuttgart: Kohlhammer, 1995).

——, 'Lord's Supper' in Freedman, D. N. (ed.) *Anchor Bible Dictionary*. 6 vols. (Garden City: Doubleday, 1992), 4:362–72.

——, *Herrenmahl und hellenistischer Kult*. Neutestamentliche Abhandlungen 15 (Münster: Aschendorffsche Verlangsbuchhandlung, 1986).

——, 'Presence in the Lord's Supper: 1 Corinthians 11:23–26 in the Context of Hellenistic Religious History' in B. F. Meyer (ed.) *One Loaf, One Cup: Ecumenical Studies of 1 Cor. 11 and Other Eucharistic Texts* (Macon, GA: Mercer University Press, 1993), pp. 57–74.

Klawek, A., *Das Gebet zu Jesus. Seine Berechtigung und Übung nach den Schriften des Neuen Testaments: Eine biblische-theologische Studie.* Neutestamentliche Abhandlungen 6/5 (Münster: Aschendorffsche Verlagsbuchhandlung, 1921).

Klein, Charlotte, *Anti-Judaism in Christian Theology*, trans. Edward Quinn (Philadelphia: Fortress Press, 1978).

Klinzing, Georg, *Die Umdeutung des Kultus in der Qumrangemeinde und im Neuen Testament* (Göttingen: Vandenhoeck & Ruprecht, 1971).

Kloppenborg, John S. and Wilson, Stephen G. (eds.) *Voluntary Associations in the Graeco-Roman World* (London: Routledge, 1996).

Kodell, Jerome, *The Eucharist in the New Testament* (Wilmington, DE: Michael Glazier, 1988).

Kraemer, Ross S. (ed.), *Maenads, Martyrs, Matrons, Monastics: A Sourcebook on Women's Religions in the Greco-Roman World* (Philadelphia: Fortress Press, 1988).

——, *Her Share of the Blessings: Women's Religions among Pagans, Jews, and Christians* (Oxford: Oxford University Press, 1992).

Kramer, Werner, *Christ, Lord, Son of God.* Studies in Biblical Theology 50 (London: SCM, 1966).

Kreitzer, L. J., *Jesus and God in Paul's Eschatology.* Journal for the Study of the New Testament Supplements 19 (Sheffield: JSOT Press, 1987).

Kroll, Joseph, *Die christliche Hymnodik bis zu Klemens von Alexandreia* (Königsberg im Breisgau: Hartungsche Buchdruckerei, 1921).

Kuhn, H.-W., *Enderwartung und gegenwärtiges Heil: Untersuchungen zu den Gemeindeliedern von Qumran* (Göttingen: Vandenhoeck & Ruprecht, 1966).

Kuhn, K. G., 'The Lord's Supper and the Communal Meal at Qumran' in Krister Stendahl (ed.), *The Scrolls and the New*

Testament (London: SCM, 1958; reprint New York: Crossroad, 1992), pp. 65–93.

Kuntzmann, Raymond, 'Le trône de Dieu dans l'oeuvre du chroniste' in Marc Philonenko (ed.), *Le Trône de Dieu*, Wissenschaftliche Untersuchungen zum Neuen Testament 69 (Tübingen: J. C. B. Mohr [Paul Siebeck], 1993), pp. 19–27.

Landsberger, Franz, 'The Sacred Direction in Synagogue and Church', *Hebrew Union College Annual* 28 (1957), pp. 181–203.

Lattke, Michael, *Hymnus: Materialien zu einer Geschichte der antiken Hymnologie*. Novum Testamentum et Orbis Antiquus 19 (Göttingen: Vandenhoeck & Ruprecht, 1991).

Lebreton, Jules, *Histoire du dogme de la trinité*. 2 vols. (Paris: Gabriel Beauchesne, 1928).

Leith, J. H., *Creeds of the Churches* (Garden City: Doubleday, 1963).

Levinskaya, Irina, *The Book of Acts in its Diaspora Setting* (Carlisle: Paternoster; Grand Rapids: Eerdmans, 1996).

Lietzmann, Hans, *Mass and Lord's Supper: A Study in the History of the Liturgy*, with 'Introduction and Further Inquiry' by R. D. Richardson, trans. D. H. G. Reeve (Leiden: Brill, 1979).

Lightfoot, J. B., Harmer, J. R., and Holmes, M. W., *The Apostolic Fathers: Greek Texts and English Translations of their Writings* (Grand Rapids: Baker, 1992²).

Lindblom, Johannes, *Prophecy in Ancient Israel* (Philadelphia: Fortress, 1962).

Lösch, Stephan, *Deitas Jesu und Antike Apotheose: Ein Beitrag zur Exegese und Religionsgeschichte* (Rottenburgh: Bader'sche Verlagsbuchhandlung, 1933).

Lortz, Joseph, 'Das Christentum als Monotheismus in den Apologien des zweiten Jahrhunderts' in Albert Michael Koeniger (ed.), *Beiträge zur Geschichte des christlichen Altertums und der Byzantinischen Literatur: Festgabe Albert Ehrhard* (Bonn/Leipzig: Kurt Schroeder, 1922), pp. 301–27.

Mach, Michael, *Entwicklungsstadien des jüdischen Engelglaubens in vorrabbinischer Zeit*. Texte und Studien zum Alten Judaismus 34 (Tübingen: J. C. B. Mohr [Paul Siebeck], 1992).

MacMullen, Ramsay, *Paganism in the Roman Empire* (New Haven: Yale University Press, 1981).

——, *Christianizing the Roman Empire, A.D. 100–400* (New Haven: Yale University Press, 1984).

MacMullen, Ramsay and Lane, Eugene N. (eds.), *Paganisn and Christianity 100–425 C.E.* (Minneapolis: Fortress Press, 1992).

Marshall, I. H., *Last Supper and Lord's Supper* (Grand Rapids: Eerdmans, 1980).

Martin, Luther H., *Hellenistic Religions: An Introduction* (New York/Oxford: Oxford University Press, 1987).

Martin, R. P., *An Early Christian Confession: Philippians 2.5–11 in Recent Interpretation* (London: Tyndale Press, 1960).

——, *Worship in the Early Church*. Rev. ed. (Grand Rapids: Eerdmans, 1973).

——, 'Worship' in G. F. Hawthorne and R. P. Martin (eds.) *Dictionary of Paul and His Letters*, (Downers Grove, Ill./Leicester, UK: InterVarsity Press, 1993), pp. 982–91.

——, 'Worship and Liturgy' in R. P. Martin and P. H. Davids (eds.) *Dictionary of the Later New Testament and its Developments* (Downers Grove, Ill.: InterVarsity, 1997), pp. 1224–38.

——, 'Some Reflections on New Testament Hymns' in H. H. Rowdon (ed.) *Christ the Lord: Studies Presented to Donald Guthrie* (Leicester: Inter-Varsity, 1982), pp. 37–49.

——, *Carmen Christi: Philippians 2:5–11 in Recent Interpretation and in the Setting of Early Christian Worship* (Cambridge: Cambridge University Press, 1967; Grand Rapids: Eerdmans, 1983[2]).

Martínez, Florentino García, *The Dead Sea Scrolls Translated: The Qumran Texts in English* (Leiden: E. J. Brill; Grand Rapids: Eerdmans, 1996[2]).

Marxsen, Willi, *The Beginnings of Christology Together with The Lord's Supper as a Christological Problem*, trans. P. J. Achtemeier and L. Nieting (Philadelphia: Fortress, 1979).

McCormick, Scot, *The Lord's Supper: A Biblical Interpretation* (Philadelphia: Westminster Press, 1966).

McGowan, A. B., ' "Is There a Liturgical Text in this Gospel?" The Institution Narratives and their Early Interpretive Communities', *Journal of Biblical Literature* 118 (1999), 73–87.

McKelvey, R. J., *The New Temple: The Church in the New Testament* (London: Oxford University Press, 1969).

McKinnon, James, *Music in Early Christian Literature* (Cambridge: Cambridge University Press, 1987).

Meeks, Wayne A., *The First Urban Christians: The Social World of the Apostle Paul* (New Haven: Yale University Press, 1983).

Meyer, Marvin W. (ed.), *The Ancient Mysteries: A Sourcebook* (San Francisco: Harper & Row, 1987).

Meyer, Marvin W. and Smith, Richard (eds.) *Ancient Christian Magic: Coptic Texts of Ritual Power* (San Francisco: HarperCollins, 1994).

Michel, Otto, 'ὁμολογεω' in G. Kittel and G. Friedrich (eds.), *Theological Dictionary of the New Testament*, trans. G. Bromiley. 10 vols. (Grand Rapids: Eerdmans, 1964–76), 5: 199–220.

Moule, C. F. D., *Worship in the New Testament* (Bramcote: Grove Books, 1983; original publication 1961).

Moulton, James Hope and Milligan, George, *The Vocabulary of the Greek Testament Illustrated from the Papyri and other Non-Literary Sources* (Grand Rapids: Eerdmans, 1972; reprint of 1930 edition). Mowry, Lucetta, 'Revelation 4–5 and Early Christian Liturgical Usage', *Journal of Biblical Literature* 71 (1952), 75–84.

Mulder, M. J. and Sysling, H. (eds.), *Mikra: Text, Translation, Reading and Interpretation of the Hebrew Bible in Ancient Judaism and Early Christianity*. CRINT 2/1 (Assen: Van Gorcum; Philadelphia: Fortress Press, 1988).

Muller, R. A., *Dictionary of Latin and Greek Theological Terms* (Grand Rapids: Baker, 1985).

Murphy, F. J., *The Religious Word of Jesus: An Introduction to Second Temple Palestinian Judaism* (Nashville: Abingdon Press, 1991).

Murphy-O'Connor, Jerome, *St. Paul's Corinth: Texts and Archaeology* (Wilmington, DE: Michael Glazier, 1983).

Neufeld, V. H., *The Earliest Christian Confessions*. New Testament Tools and Studies 5 (Grand Rapids: Eerdmans, 1963).

Nickelsburg, G. W. E. and Stone, M. E. (eds.), *Faith and Piety in Early Judaism: Texts and Documents* (Philadelphia: Fortress Press, 1983).

Nielen, J. M., *Gebet und Gottesdienst im Neuen Testament* (Freiburg im Breisgau: Herder, 1937).

Nock, A. D., *Conversion: The Old and the New in Religion from Alexander the Great to Augustine of Hippo* (Oxford: Oxford University Press, 1933; reprints 1952, 1961).

——, *Early Gentile Christianity and its Hellenistic Background* (New York: Harper & Row, 1964).

Noll, S. F., 'Angelology in the Qumran Texts' (Unpublished Ph.D. thesis, University of Manchester, 1979).

Old, H. O., 'The Psalms of Praise in the Worship of the New Testament Church' *Interpretation* 39 (1985), 20–33.

Osborn, Eric, *The Emergence of Christian Theology* (Cambridge: Cambridge University Press, 1993).

Ovadiah, A., 'The Art of the Ancient Synagogues in Israel' in Dan Urman and Paul V. M. Flesher (eds.), *Ancient Synagogues: Historical Analysis and Archaeological Discovery*. 2 vols. Studia Post-Biblica 47 (Leiden: Brill, 1995), 2:301–18.

Payne, P. B., 'Fuldensis, Sigla for Variants in Vaticanus, and 1 Cor. 14:34–35', *New Testament Studies* 41 (1995), 240–62.

Perrot, Charles, 'The Reading of the Bible in the Ancient Synagogue' in M. J. Mulder and H. Sysling (eds.), *Mikra: Text, Translation, Reading and Interpretation of the Hebrew Bible in Ancient Judaism and Early Christianity*. CRINT 2/1 (Assen: Van Gorcum; Philadelphia: Fortress Press, 1988), pp. 137–59.

Peterson, Erik, 'Die geschichtlichen Bedeutung der jüdischen Gebetsrichtung' in E. Peterson, *Frühkirche, Judentum und Gnosis: Studien und Untersuchungen.* (Rome: Herder, 1959), pp. 1–14.

Pettersen, Alvyn, *Athanasius* (London: Geoffrey Chapman, 1995).

Piper, Otto A., 'The Apocalypse of John and the Liturgy of the Ancient Church', *Church History* 20 (1951), 10–22.

Price, S. R. F., *Rituals and Power: The Roman Imperial Cult in Asia Minor* (Cambridge: Cambridge University Press, 1984).

Quasten, Johannes, *Musik und Gesang in den Kulten der heidnischen Antike und christlichen Frühzeit* (Münster: Aschendorffsche Verlagsbuchhandlung, 1973²; original edition 1930).

Reif, Stefan C., *Judaism and Hebrew Prayer: New Perspectives on Jewish Liturgical History* (Cambridge: Cambridge University Press, 1993).

Richardson, Neil, *Paul's Language about God*. Journal for the Study of the New Testament Supplements 99 (Sheffield: Sheffield Academic Press, 1994).

Roberts, Alexander and Donaldson, James (eds.), *The Ante-Nicene Fathers. 10 vols.* (New York: Christian Literature Publishing Co., 1885; reprint edition, Peabody, Mass.: Hendrickson , 1994.)

Robinson, James M. (ed.), *The Nag Hammadi Library in English*, rev. ed. (Leiden: E. J. Brill, 1988).

Rohde, Edvard, 'Gottesglaube und Kyriosglaube bei Paulus', *Zeitschrift für die Neutestamentliche Wissenschaft* 22 (1923), 43–57.

Safrai, S. and Stern, M. (eds.), *The Jewish People in the First Century: Historical Geography, Political History, Social, Cultural and Religious Life and Institutions*, vol. 2 (Assen: Van Gorcum; Philadelphia: Fortress Press, 1976).

Safrai, S., 'Religion in Everyday Life' in S. Safrai and M. Stern (eds.), pp. 793–833.

Saffrey, H. D., 'The Piety and Prayers of Ordinary Men and Women in Late Antiquity' in A. H. Armstrong (ed.), *Classical Mediterranean Spirituality: Egyptian, Greek, Roman* (New York: Crossroad, 1986), pp. 195–213.

Sanders, E. P., *Judaism: Practice and Belief, 63 BCE – 66 CE* (London: SCM; Philadelphia: Trinity Press International, 1992).

Sanders, J. T., *The New Testament Christological Hymns: Their Historical Religious Background.* Society for New Testament Studies Monograph Series 15 (Cambridge: Cambridge University Press, 1971).

Schaff, Philip., *The Creeds of Christendom.* 3 vols. (New York: Harper and Row, 1919; reprint, Grand Rapids: Baker, 1977⁶).

Schiffman, L. H., *Reclaiming the Dead Sea Scrolls* (New York: Doubleday, 1994).

——, *The Eschatological Community of the Dead Sea Scrolls.* Society of Biblical Literature Monograph Series 38 (Atlanta: Scholars Press, 1989).

Schille, G. *Frühchristliche Hymnen* (Berlin: Evangelische Verlagsanstalt, 1965).

Schillington, V. George, 'Atonement Texture in 1 Corinthians 5.5', *Journal for the Study of the New Testament* 71 (1998), 29–50.

Schmidt, K. L., 'ἐκκλησια' in G. Kittel and G. Friedrich (eds.), *Theological Dictionary of the New Testament*, trans. G. Bromiley. 10 vols. (Grand Rapids: Eerdmans, 1964–76), 3:501–36.

——, 'θρησκείαν, etc', Theological Dictionary of the New Testament. 3:155–59.

——, 'ἐπικαλεω', Theological Dictionary of the New Testament. 3:496–500.

Schmitt, J. J., 'Prophecy (Pre-exilic Hebrew)' in Freedman, D. N. (ed.) *Anchor Bible Dictionary.* 6 vols. (Garden City: Doubleday, 1992), 5:482–89.

Schowalter, D. N., *The Emperor and the Gods*, Harvard Dissertations in Religion 28 (Minneapolis: Fortress Press, 1993).

Schürer, E., *The History of the Jewish People in the Age of Jesus Christ.* Revised and edited by G. Vermes, F. Millar, and M. Goodman (Edinburgh: T. & T. Clark, 1979–86).

Segal, Alan F., *Two Powers in Heaven: Early Rabbinic Reports about Christianity and Gnosticism* (Leiden: Brill, 1977).

Sherwin-White, A. N., *The Letters of Pliny* (Oxford: Clarendon, 1966).

Smith, D. E., 'Greco-Roman Meal Customs', 'Greco-Roman Sacred Meals' in Freedman, D. N. (ed.) *Anchor Bible Dictionary*. 6 vols. (Garden City: Doubleday, 1992), 4: 650–54.

Smith, William S., *Musical Aspects of the New Testament* (Amsterdam: Uitgeverij W. Ten Have, 1962).

Sparks, H. F. D., *The Apocryphal Old Testament* (Oxford: Clarendon Press, 1984).

Stählin, G., 'Φιλεω in G. Kittel and G. Friedrich (eds.), *Theological Dictionary of the New Testament*, trans. G. Bromiley. 10 vols. (Grand Rapids: Eerdmans, 1964–76), 9:118–46.

Steenburg, David, 'The Worship of Adam and Christ as the Image of God', *Journal for the Study of the New Testament* 39 (1990), 95–109.

Strathmann, H., 'λατρεύω, λατρεία' in G. Kittel and G. Friedrich (eds.), *Theological Dictionary of the New Testament*, trans. G. Bromiley. 10 vols. (Grand Rapids: Eerdmans, 1964–76), 4:58–65.

Strathmann, H. and Meyer, R., 'Λειτουργεω, λειτουργία' in G. Kittel and G. Friedrich (eds.), *Theological Dictionary of the New Testament*, trans. G. Bromiley. 10 vols. (Grand Rapids: Eerdmans, 1964–76), 4:215–31.

Stuckenbruck, Loren T., *Angel Veneration and Christology*. Wissenschaftliche Untersuchungan zum Neuen Testament 2/70 (Tübingen: J. C. B. Mohr [Paul Siebeck], 1995).

Talmon, Shemaryahu, 'The Emergence of Institutionalised Prayer in Israel in the Light of the Qumran Literature' in M. Delcor (ed.), *Qumran. Sa piété, sa théologie, et sa milieu* (Leuven: Leuven University Press, 1978), pp. 265–84.

Taylor, Lily Ross, *The Divinity of the Roman Emperor*. American Philological Association Monograph Series 1 (Middletown, Conn.: American Philological Association, 1931; reprint Chico, Calif.: Scholars Press, n.d).

Teixidor, Javier, *The Pagan God: Popular Religion in the Greco-Roman Near East* (Princeton: Princeton University Press, 1977).

Thompson, L. L., 'Hymns in Early Christian Worship', *Anglican Theological Review* 55 (1973), 458–72.

Thraede, K., 'Ursprung und Formen des "hl. Kuss" in frühen Christentum', *Jahrbuch für Antike und Christenum* 11/12 (1968–69), 124–80.

Thüsing, Wilhelm, *Per Christum in Deum: Studien zum Verhältnis von Christozentrik und Theozentrik in den paulinischen Hauptbriefen.* Neutestamentliche Abhandlungen 1 (Münster: Aschendorffschen Verlagsbuchhandlung, 1965).

Torrance, James B., *Worship, Community, and the Triune God of Grace* (Carlisle: Paternoster, 1996).

Tov, Emmanuel, 'The Septuagint' in M. J. Mulder and H. Sysling (eds.) *Mikra: Text, Translation, Reading and Interpretation of the Hebrew Bible in Ancient Judaism and Early Christianity.* CRINT 2/1 (Assen: Van Gorcum; Philadelphia: Fortress Press, 1988), pp. 161–88.

Ulansey, David, *The Origins of the Mithraic Mysteries* (New York/Oxford: Oxford University Press, 1989).

——, 'Solving the Mithraic Mysteries', *Biblical Archaeology Review* 20 (Sept/Oct 1994), 41–53.

Urman, Dan, and Flesher, Paul V. M. (eds.), *Ancient Synagogues: Historical Analysis and Archaeological Discovery.* 2 vols. (Leiden: Brill, 1995).

Vielhauer, Philip, *Aufsätze zum Neuen Testament* (Munich: Christian Kaiser, 1965).

Wedderburn, A. J. M., *Baptism and Resurrection: Studies in Pauline Theology against its Graeco-Roman Background.* Wissenschaftliche Untersuchungen zum Neuen Testament 44 (Tübingen: J. C. B. Mohr [Paul Siebeck], 1987).

Wengst, Klaus, *Christologische Formeln und Lieder des Urchristenums* (Gütersloh: Gerd Mohn, 1972).

White, John L., 'New Testament Epistolary Literature in the Framework of Ancient Epistolography' in H. Temporini and W. Haase (eds.) *Aufstieg und Niedergang der römischen Welt* (Berlin: De Gruyter), 2. 25/2: 1730–56.

White, L. Michael, *Building God's House in the Roman World: Architectural Adaptation among Pagans, Jews, and Christians* (Baltimore: Johns Hopkins University Press, 1990).

Wiles, Maurice,. *The Making of Christian Doctrine: A Study in the Principles of Early Doctrinal Development* (Cambridge: Cambridge University Press, 1967).

Williams, Michael Allen, *Rethinking "Gnosticism": An Argument for Dismantling a Dubious Category* (Princeton: Princeton University Press, 1996).

Winter, Bruce W., 'Acts and Roman Religion' in David W. J. Gill and Conrad Gempf (eds.) *The Book of Acts in its Graeco-Roman Setting* (Carlisle: Paternoster; Grand Rapids: Eerdmans, 1994), pp. 79–103.

Wu, J. L., 'Liturgical Elements' in G. F. Hawthorne and R. P. Martin (eds.) *Dictionary of Paul and His Letters* (Downers Grove, Ill./Leicester, UK: InterVarsity Press, 1993), pp. 557–60.

Yerkes, Royden K., *Sacrifice in Greek and Roman Religions and Early Judaism* (London: A. & C. Black, 1953).